CONTEMPORARY ART WITH WOOD

creative techniques and appreciation

OTHER ART BOOKS BY DONA Z. MEILACH

DIRECT METAL SCULPTURE
  with Donald Seiden

COLLAGE AND FOUND ART
  with Elvie Ten Hoor

CREATING ART FROM ANYTHING

CREATING WITH PLASTER

MAKING RUGS AND WALL HANGINGS

PAPERCRAFT

PRINTMAKING

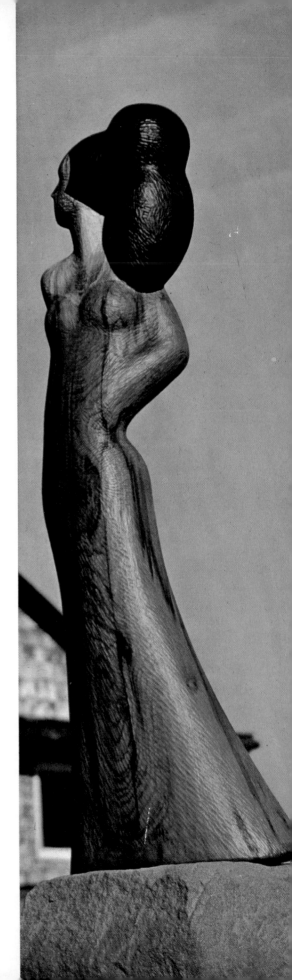

GOLD DRESS. David Hostetler.
Elm colored with aniline dye. 48″ high.
Collection, Mrs. Harry Lynde Bradley, Milwaukee.
Photo, artist

UNTITLED. Gerald J. Tomany. 1967.
Butternut, Red Oak, Poplar. 8″ × 17″ × 9″.
Photo, author

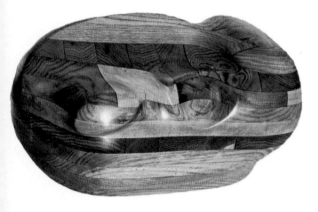

CONTEMPORARY ART WITH WOOD

creative techniques and appreciation

by DONA Z. MEILACH

CROWN PUBLISHERS, INC.   NEW YORK

Dedicated to
Rose Don Zweigoron

731.462
M47c

64072

December, 1968

Acknowledgments

Much of the satisfaction of compiling this book has come from my association with and the cooperation of hundreds of people.

I am indebted to all the artists who supplied photographs and permitted me to take photos. All received credit where their illustrations appear. My special thanks to those who allowed my camera and tape recorder to capture their demonstrations, techniques, and general philosophy about their work. All were enthusiastic and generous with time, information, and assistance.

I am grateful to the museum and gallery directors who researched their collections for sculptures made of wood. Private collectors and industry and wood associations were also anxious to help.

Schoolteachers and students welcomed me to their classrooms, and even created projects that might fit within the scope of the book.

My deep appreciation to the following for their invaluable help during the preparation of the manuscript: Ray Pearson, Illinois Institute of Technology, Institute of Design; Robert Borcherdt, Eldon Danhausen, Forman Onderdonk, and Donald Seiden, The Art Institute of Chicago; P. L. Musick, lumber expert; Seymour Zweigoron, engineer; Ben Lavitt, Astra-Photo Service; Marilyn Regula, typist; and Dr. Melvin Meilach, my husband, whose encouragement, understanding, and patience never cease to amaze me.

To my editor, Brandt Aymar, and his staff, I extend my continuing admiration for their ability to put my visualization of a book into print so efficiently.

DONA Z. MEILACH

Lincolnwood, Illinois

Contents

Acknowledgments   v

List of Color Plates   ix

PART I—SCULPTURE

chapter 1. ART WITH WOOD   3

chapter 2. WOOD AND TOOLS ... AND
HOW TO USE THEM   35

chapter 3. PAINTING AND FINISHING WOOD   57

chapter 4. LAMINATING, JOINING, PEGGING   67

chapter 5. DIRECT CARVING   91

chapter 6. ASSEMBLAGE OF FOUND AND
WEATHERED WOOD   121

chapter 7. WOOD CONSTRUCTIONS IN RELIEF   137

chapter 8. SCULPTURAL CONSTRUCTIONS—
THREE-DIMENSIONAL   147

PART II—FUNCTIONAL OBJECTS

chapter 9. ACCESSORIES   163

chapter 10. FURNITURE   177

chapter 11. WOOD, THE ARTIST, AND THE ARCHITECT   189

Glossary   204

Index   207

List of Color Plates

GOLD DRESS. David Hostetler. Elm colored with aniline dye. 48″ high.
frontispiece

UNTITLED. Gerald J. Tomany. 1967. African mahogany, Korina on black base. 10″ × 10″ × 10″.
frontispiece

EYE. John Little. 1967. Painted pine. 64″ high.
facing page 118

COCKTAIL TABLE. Robert C. Whitley. Walnut. 42″ diameter.
facing page 118

THE CANTERBURY TALES. Stanley Kaplan. Philippine mahogany carved.
facing page 118

PAINTED WOOD SCULPTURES ON EXHIBIT. Forman Onderdonk. 1966–67.
facing page 118

THIRTEEN CATS. Bernard Langlais. 1967. 48″ × 96″.
facing page 119

ASSEMBLAGE. Robert Pierron. 1967. Pine, charred and painted. 24″ × 30″.
facing page 119

THE CELLO PLAYER. Jacqueline Fogel. Found wood assemblage. 28″ high.
facing page 150

TRIAL. Don Trachsler. 1967. Painted woods.
facing page 150

DREAM IN PRIMARIES. Mychajlo R. Urban. 1967. Locust and applewood. 30″ high.
facing page 150

BUST. Ralph Noel Dagg. 1966. Black walnut. 16″ high.
facing page 151

UNTITLED. Richard Kowal. 1967. Mahogany laminated. 30″ high.
facing page 151

ICE BUCKET. Robert G. Trout. Walnut.
facing page 151

PART I— SCULPTURE

LOVE. Claude Primeau. 1965. Redwood 9′ high.

Courtesy, artist

chapter 1

Art with Wood

With the advent of modern technology and the impetus of new industrial techniques, wood is today emerging from the studios of artists in an infinite variety of forms. For centuries, wood has been associated with construction, folk art, decoration, and utilitarian objects. Ancient and primitive peoples carved idols as well as serving vessels from wood. Fifteenth- and sixteenth-century Italian and German woodcutters created intricate, beautiful altarpieces. Early American carvings were of weather vanes, ships' figures, and cigar-store Indians as well as utensils and equipment for domestic and industrial use.

Today, wood is becoming an important medium for the creative artist as well as the craftsman, artisan, and builder. The sculptor is exploiting its potential to create works that exhibit pent-up energy, power, and an intense expressiveness independent of the objects they may represent.

Those who work with wood invariably speak of a deep emotional involvement with the material itself. Wood is warm, alive. It has texture, grain, color, and aroma. It yields to the chisel and gouge more easily than do marble and other stones.

But working with wood today is not confined to traditional carving with chisels and gouges. Today's artists often use the tools of industry, such as power saws and acetylene torches, to build, assemble, and construct sculptures that comment distinctively on our contemporary environment. It is this, perhaps, that is most responsible for the changing role of wood in contemporary art.

Wood has burst its way out of sculpture carved from a log. As the artist adapts industrial techniques, he may glue several pieces of wood together until the resulting shape has little or no resemblance to the original cylindrical tree trunk. He is likely to abandon age-old human and animal forms for abstractions and disquieting images that avoid realism.

Until the last few decades most sculptures were of stones, such as marble and granite, or metals, such as bronze, silver, and iron. These media lasted for centuries, while the tendency of wood was to deteriorate slowly. This is because wood is an organic substance; stone and metal are inorganic. Even after a tree is cut and cured, it expands, contracts, and weathers because of changes of temperature and humidity. A form carved from a log may crack or "check" as it dries out. Warpage, the direction of the grain, knots, and the instability of wood outdoors make it a comparatively unreliable art medium. Because artists felt it unwise to use material with unpredictable and uncontrollable physical properties—and uncertain durability—they adhered to more permanent and dependable materials.

4

PAINTED WOOD FIGURE.
3rd Century, B.C.
Ch'ang-Sha.

*Courtesy, Art Institute
of Chicago*

FIGURE OF A NEGRO PREACHER ON A CHAIR,
HOLDING A BOOK. American sculpture. 19th
century.

*Courtesy, Art Institute of Chicago.
Collection, Vaughan Fund*

Today, however, sculptors' attitudes about the vicissitudes of wood differ. Many believe that checks in a log are the nature of the material, and are to be used or avoided as best suits the artist's purpose. Others believe checking can be minimized by proper handling. Those who object to checks in logs may work with boards that have been air- or kiln-dried by commercial methods.

World trade and modern technology are largely responsible for increased artistic activity with wood in recent years. As trade routes expanded, exotic woods from South America, Africa, Asia, and other parts of the world became available. The sculptor found great variety in woods of density, grain, and color differing from those in his immediate locale. Such varying characteristics became the beauty and challenge of the material, and afforded the artist pleasure in working with it.

Technological developments by the lumber industry in the past few decades have made rapid drying of wood possible. Boards once required three years to air-dry; now effi-cient kilns accomplish effective drying in hours. Products that combine wood with resins are being introduced. Such products are dimensionally stable; they never change measurements because of weather, and can be cut and tooled like wood. Used commercially for building, for signs, and other purposes, they are being brought into art schools for experimentation.

As sculptors take advantage of the tools of industry, their output often accelerates. A chain saw, for example, enables an artist to strip bark and sapwood from a tree trunk in an hour or so, while removal by hand with an ax means a week or more of artistically unproductive hard labor. The accessibility and efficiency of power tools, dependable glues, and finishes all contribute to the increasing use of wood in the arts.

When you begin to work with wood, it's a good idea to become familiar with the nature of the material and its limitations. You may gouge, chisel, saw, nail, carve, scorch, and glue wood. You will quickly discover that grain,

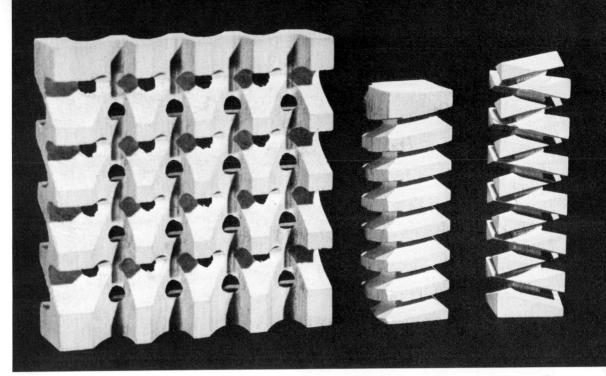

Planks and blocks of wood are cut with an ordinary table saw to create these striking designs in wood. By raising, lowering, and angling the saw blade, and cutting in from front, back, or sides, students quickly learn to produce an infinite variety of such forms.

Photos, author

knots, density, dryness, and type of wood are factors that must be recognized.

The examples in this book have been developed by students and professional artists, by primitive and sophisticated cultures. The reader should remember that there is no absolute way to use wood. Each artist develops his own style and methods that may be right for him. Those who have unselfishly shared their techniques emphasize the importance of trying everything with wood, and then deciding what methods best serve to express their individualities.

Beginning students in design classes create three-dimensional, nonrepresentational wood designs as they become familiar with saws and drills. They are usually amazed that builders' tools and materials can be used imaginatively within only a few minutes after the student learns to use the equipment.

Examples by students, Institute of Design, I.I.T., Chicago. Ray Pearson, Instructor

Circles of plywood are cut off center with a band saw and reassembled into new relationships by gluing. Flat pieces of wood are thus given three-dimensional sculptural form.

FRAGMENTATION

Familiar objects, wood dowels, and molding strips are cut and reassembled by students as they learn to use a band saw. The student learns to divorce an object from its original use and give it new form. This technique, called "fragmentation" by Ray Pearson, can be an unbounded creative experience. Students are cautioned not to imitate, but to initiate their own creations.

Students, Institute of Design,
I.I.T., Chicago

A table-tennis paddle and ball fragmented. The first few attempts will be more successful if the cuts are well planned and orderly.

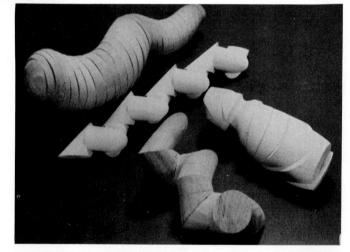

These odd shapes were created by sawing and reconstructing a wood club and dowels of different sizes. They are joined by gluing.

Ruler fragmented. Also try fragmenting wooden kitchen items such as stirring spoons, cutting boards, rolling pins, and salad bowls.

Photos, author

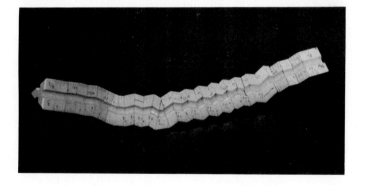

FINDING RELATIONSHIPS

Sculptor Fred Borcherdt has created a set of basic wooden forms with which he experiments to find new relationships between geometrical solids. By constantly rearranging, by adding some shapes and removing others, Borcherdt discovers stimulating ideas for sculptures. These forms were made from scrap wood. Some remain in their natural tones; others are waxed, stained, or painted. The constantly changing relationships of finishes and types of wood also present idea images.

Begin with random shapes such as these, and develop infinite arrangements.

Anyone can develop a similar set of sculptural "blocks" and build with them until they suggest pleasing forms.
Photos, author

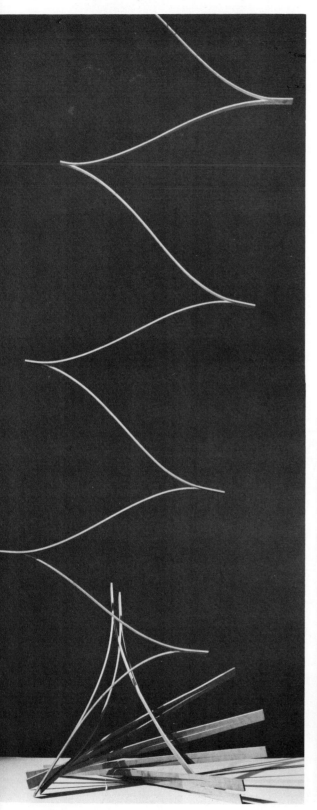

One normally doesn't think of wood as having "stretchable" qualities. Yet, by creative cutting with a jigsaw, these originally flat pieces of birch plywood have actually been stretched. Cutting should be practiced on paper first.

Birch plywood project. James Prestini. Single-ply birch cut, as in drawing below to within an inch of each edge, then arranged, stretched, and held at top.

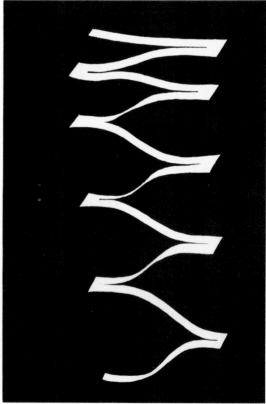

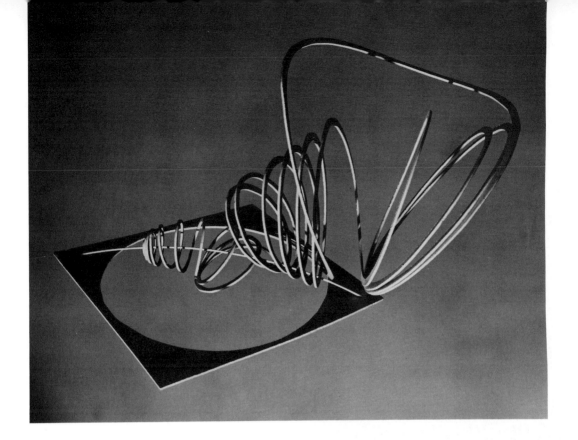

Birch plywood project. James Prestini. A continuous circular strip cut from a square of 3-ply birch. It remains attached at one end, and the spiral form is arranged on a dowel, arched, and tacked to the base.

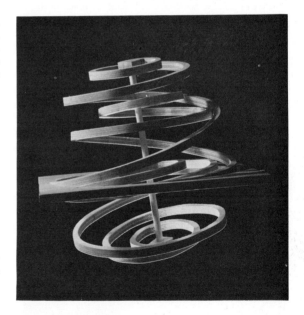

Photos, Barbara Morgan

Birch plywood project. James Prestini. A wide circular strip is cut from 5-ply birch. That strip is cut again. It is stretched and held apart with a dowel. Three cuts were made here, with two strips at the top and one pulled to the bottom.

UNTITLED. Arnold Cherullo. Pine boxes with protruding shapes painted with black and white acrylics. Boxes are designed to be arranged by viewer.

Courtesy, artist

SHAPE AND VARIATION. John Randall Kabot. A project that required three possible variations from a basic rectangular block has parts that move in and out. Shown are the block and one variation, with another indicated at left side.

Student, University of Illinois at the Chicago Circle. John Walley, instructor

PIGEONHOLING. Bernard Langlais. 1962. 72″ high × 48″ wide. Scraps of wood assembled as both inlay and relief.

Courtesy, Allan Stone Gallery, New York

SIMO SOCIETY HEADDRESS. Baga Tribe, Guinea. Total headdress 47″ high. Head portion of a huge mask fits over the shoulders and was worn by the dancers of the Simo Society during fertility ceremonies. The shapes are simplified, or stylized, by today's terminology, with intricate surface carvings. There is a repeat of circular and semicircular shapes in the nose, the ear, the forehead piece, the eye, and the decorations.

Courtesy, Art Institute of Chicago

LINTEL used over doorway. North Central Coast,
Peru. 1300–1500 A.D. 54″ long.
Courtesy, Art Institute of Chicago

HELMET MASK. Senufo Tribe, Korhogo District, Ivory Coast. 40⅛″ long.
These helmets, called "fire-spitter masks," were used in rituals to drive
away soul-eaters. They included many different animal forms. Parts were
put together with vine ties or hide glues.
Courtesy, Art Institute of Chicago

When we consider that wood has been used for so many centuries in so many ways, it is impossible to select a point in time when it became an important medium in contemporary art. One can only follow the history of sculpture, observe the materials used, and speak with sculptors who have worked with wood for many years.

In the early 1900's, Western artists were seeking an escape from the prevalent romantic and pictorial representation of the day. They were looking for more fundamental art expression. The answer was found in the primitive carvings being brought to the Western world from Africa, Samoa, and other distant coun-

tries. These carvings, by people of primitive cultures, were blissfully simple and unaffected by the formal theories of esthetics that were strangling Western art. The primitive carver did a straightforward job of carving the available material. Often he sat so the sun came over his shoulder and outlined broad, simple planes. Details were usually suggested with surface treatment.

As primitive carvings circulated, Western artists borrowed from these sources in a frankly eclectic manner. The impact was tremendous. Bronze and stone sculptures by Pablo Picasso and Constantin Brancusi first reflected this simplicity. Picasso's early experimenting with

14

WOMAN WITH MANTILLA. Henri Laurens. 1915. Painted wood construction. 12″ high. Though Laurens used wood, he also made similar Cubist statements in stone and sheet metal. Though wood, at this time, was being explored, it was not yet considered a vital material for expression.

Collection, Mr. and Mrs. Arnold Maremont,
Chicago

KING OF KINGS. Constantin Brancusi. Exact date unknown. 118″ high. Brancusi sought simplified forms, and was greatly influenced by primitive sculptures. He believed in "truth of materials," and ignored the checking that appeared in wood.

Courtesy, Solomon R. Guggenheim
Museum, New York

wood in cubist forms were three carvings made in 1907. By 1914, Picasso had delved into collage and assemblage, using wood for all or many of the parts.

Following World War I, artists became concerned with the machine and its effect upon the times. The Futurists emphasized the machine age as an esthetic ideal in painting and sculptures. The concept was strengthened after 1918 by a group of Moscow artists who applied engineering principles to sculpture. The movement, entitled "Constructivism" because of the architectural feeling of the construc-

tions, encouraged a new interest in spatial relationships. The Constructivists attempted to destroy volume and replace it by concave or transparent form, often using negative spaces. Materials were chosen from among those most typical of the industrial environment: metal, plastics, and wood. Constructivism was the first coherent attempt to create an abstract art of three instead of two dimensions, and wood was an easily available material to use for this purpose.

Traditional carving certainly was not abandoned, but it did undergo change. Ernst Barlach, a German sculptor, created carved pieces that were quite different from the ex-

BIRDS IN AN AQUARIUM. Jean Arp. C. 1920. 9⅞″ × 8″. Arp's early use of wood was with undulating shapes cut out of thick board and placed one above the other in two, three, or four tiers. They were positioned to be complementary or discordant to one another. They were painted.

Courtesy, Museum of Modern Art, New York

THE HORSE. Alexander Calder. 1928. Walnut. 34¾″ long. The horizontal wood grain is used to increase the feeling of an elongated body. The carved features and lightly scratched texture present an extremely simplified and even humorous statement of the animal. Note how unrealistically, yet effectively, the body is set into the legs.

Courtesy, Museum of Modern Art, New York. Lillie P. Bliss Bequest

LILLIAN LEITZEL. Chaim Gross. 1938. Carved in Macassar ebony. 52″ high. Natural wood color adds beauty to the form. Gross's female figures are solid, with narrow waists and ankles and broad hips. He believes in using not only gouges and chisels but any kind of tool to achieve the infinite variety of configurations. He prefers to work from solid pieces of log.

Collection, Metropolitan Museum of Art, New York

WOODEN IMAGE. Yoruba Tribe, Nigeria, Africa. Such simple circular negative space formed within the hand may have been the inspiration for the interior uses of space by sculptors in the 1930's.

Courtesy, Smithsonian Institution, Washington, D.C.

MOTHER AND CHILD. Henry Moore. 1938. Elmwood. 30⅜" high. Moore combined forms of different sizes in one sculpture. He created abstract spaces within the sculpture very different from traditional negative areas between arms and legs that appeared in earlier sculptures.

Courtesy, Museum of Modern Art, New York.
Lillie P. Bliss Bequest

Two Forms. Henry Moore. 1934. Pynkado wood. 11" high.

*Collection, Museum of Modern Art,
New York. Gift of Sir Michael Sadler*

tremely pictorial, decorative work being produced by his contemporaries. Barlach rejected the classical forms in favor of more simplified and powerful depersonalized human figures.

Henri Laurens created wooden constructions in the Cubist style. And Jean Arp applied wood boards to one another to obtain tiers of undulating forms used by the Dadaists. During this period, ideas were more important than materials; wood, considered structural, was most often painted. In most instances the form could have been effectively produced in sheet metal, marble, or bronze; but wood was less expensive and more easily obtainable.

Chaim Gross discovered that exotic woods used by furniture makers and interior decorators were a neglected carving material. Rosewood, teak, ebony, and other beautiful hardwoods had lasted for years; why not use these for sculpture? He found that such woods were available from industrial sources, and he explored their properties. Instead of logs indigenous to his area, he could now use woods of varying density, texture, and color. He could depend on the tones and grains of the wood to lend more excitement to the overall image. The forms became at once even more beautiful, sensual, and expressive when the inherent qualities of the wood were subtly subordinated to the form. Though Gross designed primarily

LARGE AND SMALL FORM. Barbara Hepworth. 1945. Cornish elm. 24½″ high.
Courtesy, Marlborough-Gerson Gallery, Inc.,
New York

to take advantage of the cylindrical log shape, other sculptors began to seek the unusual woods for laminations and constructions. Gross maintains that "one should strive for beauty of form and let the natural beauty of the wood remain secondary in importance."

By the 1930's sculptural invention was pervading the art scene in the United States and in Europe. Henry Moore radically advanced wood carving from naturalistic and representational to abstract, retaining all the necessary elements of sculpture—volume, mass, space, and formal coherence. Moore often worked smaller pieces in wood, even translating them into bronze or stone for out-

door use. He penetrated materials to emphasize interior space within a form. He found he could do this easily with wood. He also began to relate and combine several different sizes, sections, and directions of form into an organic whole.

Barbara Hepworth used wood more profusely than her contemporary, Henry Moore. Beginning about 1953, her sculptures were created from rosewood, Spanish mahogany, Nigerian wood, beechwood, sandalwood, boxwood, teak, and local elmwood. Hepworth's early sculptures were smooth and unpainted, relying completely on form, texture, and grain. Later, she combined smooth areas with roughly carved areas. Still later, she defined some of the carved areas with paint. She had also used wood to create kinetic sculptures.

Hepworth's sculptures often give the feeling she had to work from the inside out rather than the outside in. Both she and Moore have a kind of magical sense about the materials they use and how they use them. Hepworth once wrote about the exciting, wondrous feeling she had while carving a heavy, dark mass of African wood. She described its particular tropical animal odor and how great a discovery it seemed to penetrate into the wood and let light fall on what was formerly dark and hidden from light.

By the early and middle 1950's wood appeared in almost every important sculpture show. It became apparent that artists were designing for wood and discovering that it was better adaptable to certain forms than marble or metal. An astonishing variety of techniques were evident: carving, assembling, constructing, laminating, and combinations. The sculptures were made of everything from exotic woods to weathered old railroad ties. They represented a wide stylistic range. Some were boldly designed; many emulated sculpture made of metal; there were obvious machine-age, human, animal, organic, and abstract themes.

As the artist continues to explore the world of wood, he finds there is much to be learned about it. He must seek new sources for his materials; he must master the tools and techniques required to achieve the forms he visualizes. Often, solutions to his construction and finishing problems are not to be found in the local hardware store or lumberyard, but in the resources of industry. Ideally, he is oriented toward science and engineering, and in solving his problems he can take advantage of the latest technological developments. Yet

RELIEF. Ben Nicholson. 1939. Painted wood. 32⅞" × 45".

*Courtesy, Museum of Modern Art,
New York. Gift of H. S. Ede and the artist*

he must know where to draw the line between a work that is admired for its form rather than for its technology.

The artist must be familiar with the nature of wood. He will discover, for example, that a log cut in the springtime and running with sap is quite different to work with than the same log cut in the wintertime. He will observe the effects of changes of temperature and humidity on wood. He will learn how a tree grows, and what causes crotches, knots, and burls, and how these can be utilized. Like a botanist, he may learn to recognize a genus by its leaf, its fruit, or its bark.

Today, artists work in many media, and move easily from stone to metal to wood. A few, such as Anne Arnold and Louise Nevelson, design solely for wood, but that does not mean they always have or always will. The artist continually experiments, and is often an innovator. He is discovering that wood can be adapted to an unending variety of forms and visual effects encompassing the emotional, mystical, and spiritual needs of the artist.

To understand, appreciate, and create art with wood, it is necessary to expand your knowledge and observations of many things in your daily life. Once you become familiar with wood, you will have a new awareness of its use in sculpture, in furniture, in fences, in the interiors and exteriors of buildings, or in useful objects such as bowls and furniture. You will discover a new beauty in the textures and shapes of pieces of wood that have been weathered by sand, sun, and water.

Artistically, the possibilities and uses of wood are still being explored. The techniques that follow, and the infinite range of content and form, are offered to increase your appreciation of wood and to stimulate your own creative endeavors with this ancient yet "new" medium of art.

FAMILY OF FIVE ACROBATS. Chaim Gross. 1955. Mahogany. 14' high. Though carved from a plank only 2" deep, it gives a feeling of roundness and depth.

Courtesy, artist. Photo, John D. Schiff

As the use of wood in sculpture followed contemporary trends, it became a potent force for expressing emotions. The theme, form, texture, and finish all became integrated concepts.

SANCTUARY. Bunni Sovetski. Elm. 1952. *Collection, Virginia Kast, Chicago. Photo, Paul Hansen*

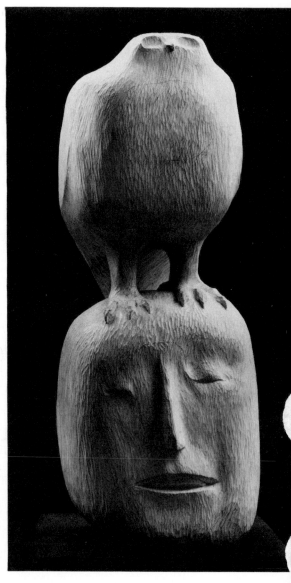

OPPRESSED MAN. Leonard Baskin. 1960. Pine painted white. 31″ high, 13″ wide, 11½″ deep. *Collection, Whitney Museum of American Art, New York*

L'ENFLURE. Roel D'Haese. 1962.
Cherry-wood. 27″ × 12″.
Courtesy, Galerie Claude Bernard, Paris

OEDIPUS AS A YOUNG BOY. Sidney Simon. 1960.
Laminated black walnut and iron. 34″ high, 12″
wide. The artist says: "This sculpture stands for
an angry young boy who is hostile . . . an image
created by a generation concerned with air-raid
shelters and wars."

Collection, Mrs. Arthur Hadley, Jr., New York

LIFE AND EARTH. Augustin Cardenas. 1957. 19″ high.
Collection, Mr. and Mrs. Arnold Maremont,
Winnetka, Illinois

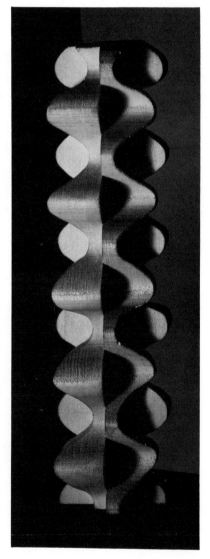

FIR SCULPTURE. James Prestini. 12′ high.
Photo, Barbara Morgan

Oval. James Faralla. 1961. Wood construction painted white. 72″ × 48″. Gradually, the use of wood scraps and weathered-wood assemblages grew in artistic importance. The concept of sculpture altered to include three-dimensional reliefs as well as "in the round" pieces that could be viewed from all sides.

Courtesy, San Francisco Museum of Art.
Gift of the Women's Board

WET MEADOW. Hans Hokanson. Redwood. 74″ high, 44″ wide, 18″ deep.
Carved and assembled pieces of redwood, which can endure weathering
without deterioration, jut perilously into space.
Courtesy, Fischbach Gallery, New York. Photo, Val Telberg

By the 1960's wood sculptures utilized themes and materials expressive of the sculptor's existence. His themes often have symbolic references. The images may be solely part of the artist's emotional and physical environment, as opposed to classical images.

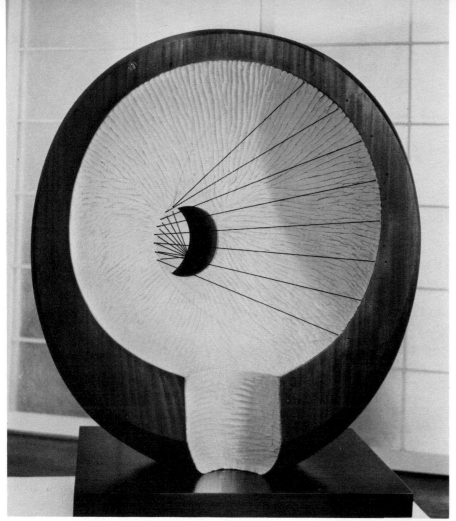

Pierced Hemisphere (Telstar). Barbara Hepworth. 1963. Guarea wood. 36½″ high. The gouged textured areas are painted, and contrast with the smooth exterior shell of the natural wood. A linear quality is added with the heavy string or wire at front and rear of sculpture.

Courtesy, Marlborough-Gerson Gallery, Inc.
New York

The Tickler. Don Baum. 1962. Construction of brooms, brushes, and so on, with wood parts, shows the artist's interest in utilizing cast-off objects of his environment.

Photo, Aaron Siskind

CHELSEA REACH II. Gabriel Kohn. 1960–1961. 24½″ × 52½″. Kohn's shapes are made by laminating layers of wood and constructing them so they shoot out diagonally and horizontally into space. They are balanced on one or two points, and are architecturally engineered in their relationship to space and of the parts to one another. The type of wood Kohn uses is unimportant. Surfaces are usually smoothly sanded.

Courtesy, Marlborough-Gerson Gallery, Inc.,
New York. Photo, Rudolph Burckhardt

TRIUMVIRATE. Forman Onderdonk. 1965. Pine painted black. Constructed geometrical forms are interrelated, though separated from one another. Individually, they enclose space, yet together they have an open use of space.

Photo, author

BRIGHTS BLUFF. Sondra Beal. 1965. Wood, Liquitex, and motors. 26"
high, 26" wide, 26" deep. Kinetic sculpture combines carving, laminating,
pegging construction, and painting.

Courtesy, B. C. Holland Gallery, Chicago.
Photo, Nathan Rabin

As sculptors accepted and struggled with the challenges of wood, changes in form, concepts, and use of the material were inevitable. The lessons of earlier masters such as Rodin, Maillol, Brancusi, and Arp, the Cubists, Expressionists, and Constructivists were aspects of an education already absorbed. It was time to move on, to make new statements concerning the present. Changes involved laminating large structures, combining sculptural surface with contemporary painting, completely different and more expressive than the decorative painting of the past. Mechanical and kinetic sculptures emerged. Gluing became as important for adding woods together as carving had been for subtracting them.

ANIMAL FARM. Bernard Langlais, 1963.
96″ × 107″. Weathered woodcut, carved,
painted, and laminated in a relief sculpture.
    *Courtesy, Art Institute of Chicago. L.
Lewis Cohn Foundation restricted gift*

REFLECTIONS I. William P. Sildar. 1964.
Laminated wood, 45″ by 50″.
     *Courtesy, Sculptors Guild, Inc.,
New York*

CLOSED SILENCE. Lucio Muñoz.
1967. Wood, carved and painted.
Courtesy, Galería Juana Mordó,
Madrid

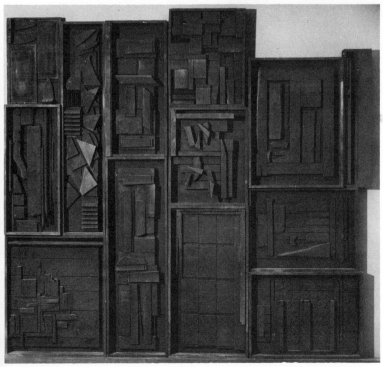

YOUNG SHADOWS. Louise Nevelson. 1959–1960. 115″ high, 126″ wide, 7¾″ deep. Discarded pieces of wood constructed within various sized boxes, and painted black. Often the wooden forms are arranged to resemble still-life and landscape motifs.
Collection, Whitney Museum of American Art, New York.
Photo, Geoffrey Clements

FROM THE MUSEUM OF SHATTERED DREAMS. H. C. Westermann. 1965. Cedar, ebony, and pine. 29″ high. In a showing entitled "Eight Sculptors: The Ambiguous Image," the introduction to Westermann's sculptures indicates that his style is isolated from the general trend and has a mysterious quality: ". . . his carefully carpentered objects contain elements which allude to the actual world, but as a whole they resist interpretations."

Collection, Walker Art Center, Minneapolis.
Photo, Eric Sutherland

FOUR ARCHES. Doris Chase. 1967. Laminated cedar with aluminum. 66″ high. As sculptors became concerned with environment, they conceived sculptures large enough for a person to walk into and through, sculptures of which they could feel a part instead of just an observer.

Courtesy, Ruth White Gallery, New York

L'ÉTÉ DE LA FORÊT. François Stahly. 1964–1966. Oak. Exhibited at the Art Institute of Chicago.

chapter 2

Wood and Tools...
and How to Use Them

All wood comes from trees. This obvious statement is probably the only precise one that can be made about wood. No matter how trees and their characteristics are categorized, there are always some trees within a species that do not conform to the general specifications. Any absolute theory concerning the best ways to work with wood would be refuted by people working with the same wood.

The growth of a tree is affected by myriad conditions such as climate, moisture, seasons, and the amount of light received. If white oak, for example, were described as tan or light brown, there would also be specimens with a distinct reddish hue.

Such variations found in just one kind of tree, multiplied by the more than 800 kinds, defies hard-and-fast definitions and descriptions. The following information is based on general knowledge and use.

SOFTWOOD AND HARDWOOD

The two major classifications for wood are "softwood" and "hardwood." Softwood comes from trees that have needlelike leaves, such as pine, fir, hemlock, holly, and all evergreens. All softwoods are nonporous, but they usually have large and open grains. The grain may or may not be conducive to natural finishing, depending upon the quality of the wood. Softwoods usually, though not always, are easy to saw, carve, and nail. Generally they are better for broad-planed sculptures than for intricate carving because they tend to split and sliver. (Pine is an exception; it cuts clean and sharp.) Softwoods are ideal for constructions that will ultimately be painted. With the exception of redwood, most softwoods tend to deteriorate more readily than hardwoods.

Hardwood comes from broad-leaved trees such as oak, walnut, mahogany, cherry, ebony, maple, and hickory. Hardwoods are close-grained, with very fine, small pores. Hence, hardwoods are often referred to as "porous" woods. Close grain inhibits splintering, which makes hardwoods desirable for carving. Hardwood pieces, properly maintained, can last for centuries.

HOW A TREE GROWS

As a tree grows from the center outward and upward, it adds layers. These layers form rings that tell the story of the tree's growth. At one time a tree's growth was "read" only after the tree was cut down and its entire cross-section observed. Today, lumbermen can take a plug from a tree in the same way that one plugs a watermelon. The plug gives various clues to the tree's growth.

GRAIN AND FIGURE

When wood is cut vertically into boards, a pattern is evident. This pattern is the grain. Grain is the actual fibrous structure of the wood. It runs the length of the tree in directions and arrangements. As the tree's growth differs seasonally, these fibers expand at different rates. Quicker growth results in a more pronounced, often unusual pattern that is referred to as the figure.

Figure in the grain is determined by (1) the way the tree grows during different seasons, (2) the part of the tree from which the wood is taken, and (3) the manner in which the wood is sawed. These may be important considerations to the sculptor who utilizes pattern.

Oak, walnut, zebrawood, and rosewood are highly figured woods that have a rapid summer growth period. Because mahogany grows at a more uniform rate through the growing season, its pattern is more regular. Ebony usually has only grain and no figure. As the tree matures, the growth rings change; therefore pieces of wood cut from low, middle, or high portions of the same tree differ greatly. If boards are cut straight (plain-sawed) or on an angle (quartersawed), the appearance of the figure will also be affected.

Unusual figuring also appears in the crotches or *V*-like areas where the trunk separates into branches. Burls, which are domelike outgrowths from the trunk caused by broken or cut branches, are highly figured because the fibers expand, compress, and encircle the growth. Knots, caused by branches breaking, often are found within the tree's trunk between and within the rings.

Two kinds of grain are evident on a length of dressed board: end grain and face grain. End grain is the result of a horizontal cut across a log. Portions of the log's rings,

Drawing of how a tree grows
Annual rings: growth circles.
Bark: a tree's "skin," or protective coating.
Cambium: living cell layer that carries food from the leaves to all parts of the tree.
Sapwood: growth layers that carry sap from roots to leaves.
Heartwood: the tree growth surrounding the pith that once was sapwood. It gives the
    tree strength.
Pith: the center from which the tree began growth.

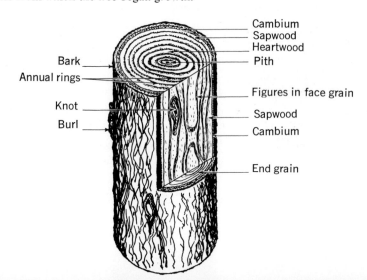

Cambium
Sapwood
Heartwood
Pith

Bark
Annual rings

Figures in face grain

Knot
Burl

Sapwood
Cambium

End grain

RED DRESS. David Hostetler. 1965. Maple. 62"
high. Close-up showing how figure, grain and knots
appear.

Courtesy, artist. Photo, Jon Webb

pith, heartwood, and sapwood appear. The face grain runs the length of the board. It is in the face grain that the most beautiful patterns appear.

Recognizing grain directions is important to the sculptor. Cutting with the grain is relatively easy because the tool is actually separating the fibers. Cutting across the grain creates resistance because the tool is compressing the fibers. When boards are laminated, the grain of each board may be placed in opposing directions for extra strength and to reduce warping. This means that the carver must use his tools in opposite ways on differing boards. Mastering the grain requires practice and experience.

How the log is used

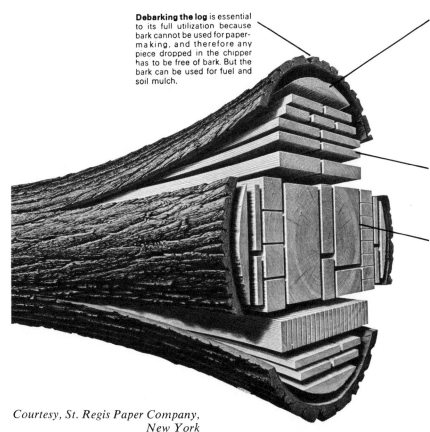

Debarking the log is essential to its full utilization because bark cannot be used for papermaking, and therefore any piece dropped in the chipper has to be free of bark. But the bark can be used for fuel and soil mulch.

The rounded sides of the log, called "slabs," are the first pieces sent to the chipper as the log goes through the sawmill. This idealized picture shows the entire log being used for lumber, except for the slabs. Actually, as cutting continues, other pieces go to the chipper, including edgings, trim ends, and other parts of the log not usable as lumber. Each log presents different problems and can be handled differently.

The outer portions of the log have the fewest knots. This "clear" lumber is usually made into boards or planks varying in thickness from one to three inches.

Toward the center of the log, knots increase and the wood is less suitable for boards. Heavier planks, and square or rectangular beams are normally sawed from this section. The center of the log is used primarily for structural beams strong enough so that they are not weakened by knots. Knots are most frequent here because this is the oldest section of the tree. Branches that were removed during the early years of the tree's life left knots that were covered over as the tree grew outward.

*Courtesy, St. Regis Paper Company,
New York*

Sculptors point out that highly figured woods are extremely attractive because of their inherent beauty. A sculptor who may be selfish about his work prefers to have a piece admired for form rather than for its natural beauty. The ideal situation is to use a beautifully figured, colored wood so deftly that its attributes enhance rather than dominate form.

COLOR

Everyone who has observed wood in furniture, wall paneling, accessories, and so on, subconsciously labels wood as light or dark. Wood color is highly variable. The surfaces of naturally light-colored woods, such as beech, holly, pine, white oak, and chestnut, may be stained to look like expensive walnut, oak, and other hardwoods (see Chapter 4). Color within one tree can differ tremendously. Poplar, for instance, has heartwood that can range from pale olive brown to yellow-brown; the sapwood is lighter. Wood within one poplar tree may also have green and purple tones.

Inherently dark woods have such rich coloring that staining defeats the reason for using the wood. Walnut, popular for furniture and unexcelled for carving, has such beautiful color and finishing properties that rarely is anything other than a coat of oil or wax applied.

SELECTING AND BUYING WOOD

The wood you select will depend on how you plan to use it, where it will be placed, its availability and cost. The easiest place to buy wood is from a lumberyard. The commoner woods are available as boards of varying lengths, widths, and grades. Certain companies specialize in rare, exotic woods for custom furniture designers and craftsmen. Their ads may be found in craft, art, and hobby magazines. Simply write for their catalogs, which contain a wealth of information about woods and suggestions for use. School industrial-arts departments may buy woods from these sources because they offer a wide variety unavailable elsewhere.

Knowing how lumber is graded will help you choose the best wood for your project most economically. If the final sculpture is to be painted, a common medium-graded wood may be adequate. If the final work will depend partly for its beauty on the color and grain of the wood, you may wish to purchase the higher grade.

After rough-sawing, lumber is sorted into different grades established by the lumber industry. The two broad classifications are "select" and "common." Select is graded A to C. Common is graded Nos. 1 to 4. Prices are related to quality.

Select

A. Top quality usually sold for furniture by specialty wood houses. The most perfect blemish-free woods.
B. Blemish-free; sometimes called "B and better."
C. Small defects such as knots, slightly torn grain, highly variable coloring.

Common

1. Contains pieces with small defects. Knots are always sound and fairly evenly distributed along a board.
2. The same type of defect as No. 1 but more of them. Most popular grade for all-around utility.
3. Numerous coarse knots or boards with loose knots and an occasional hole where knots have fallen out. Boards are less uniform in appearance than 1 and 2. Includes boards that have been improperly sawed or that

did not plane smooth on both sides. Probably the lowest grade to be considered for a project.

4. Rough, coarse, knotty wood usually used for crating.

When purchasing lumber, you will learn that the sizes of boards are not really what you ask for. A 1″ × 2″ rough board, for instance, is usually dressed to 25/32″ × 1⅝″. A 2″ × 4″ is surfaced to 1⅝″ × 3⅝″.

Lumber prices are by the board foot: a measurement that stands for a board 1″ thick, 12″ wide, and 12″ long. Transportation also plays a part in the cost of wood. One who lives near forests and mills will pay less for his lumber than one who lives farther away.

How a Tree Is Sawed.

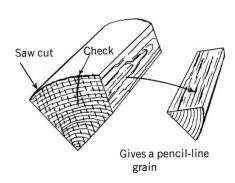

Gives a pencil-line grain

Rift-sawed

In rift-sawing, the log is trimmed to a square. Boards are cut on angles to the annual rings, and narrow toward the center. A more balanced grain pattern results.

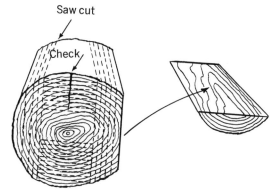

Plain-sawed

Boards are sawed from logs in different ways. The cuts are referred to as "plain," "rift," and "quartersawed." Plain-sawed lumber has less waste and is cheaper, easier to kiln-dry, and averages wider boards than other methods of sawing. It does not provide good figures, and boards tend to warp.

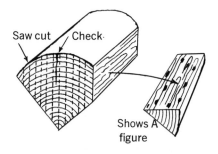

Shows A figure

Quarter-sawed

Quartersawed wood is cut on an angle to the heartwood. It shrinks and checks and splits less than wood cut by other methods of sawing. With quartersawed wood, more figuring results, and the wood is more expensive because there is more waste.

Logs are not so easy to come by as lumber. In small towns and suburban areas, trees are often cut down for land clearance. Often an artist may have a portion of a log if he will cart it away. This is more easily said than done. You may have to borrow or hire a truck, but no one ever said sculpture was easy. Tree surgeons, veneer companies, and builders are also good sources of logs.

Often an artist or cabinetmaker will find, growing on a farm, a tree that has the kind of grain and figuring he wants. He may buy the tree from the farmer and have it cut down. If he is interested in the crotch or burl areas, he may leave the stump. Another man may purchase the stump for his needs. This happens frequently, especially with walnut trees, which are rapidly diminishing in supply, and command excellent prices. Because furniture makers will pay greater prices for optimum parts of a tree, the sculptor must often settle for rejected portions. Yet knots and other defects can be magnificently manipulated within a sculptural form. (See page 90, work by Fred Borcherdt.)

It is wise to identify a log or tree correctly before you decide to buy, cut, and haul it.

There are over 800 species of trees in the United States alone. Identify local trees by leaves, fruit, and bark. Samples of 48 woods, with their characteristics and uses printed on backs, are available at a nominal cost.

*Samples, courtesy, Frank Paxton Lumber
Company, Chicago*

Refer to any of the tree identification books available in paperback and in United States Government publications. Identify the tree by bark, leaf, flower, or fruit, then check the description. If the wood is used mainly for making crates, it will not be good for sculpture. However, if the wood is used for commercial furniture, you know it can be used for sculpture. A serious sculptor may own or rent a chain saw, and once he gets permission he may cut a tree down himself. A trunk that cuts easily with a chain saw should be easy to carve.

Used woods are less trouble to get and less expensive than new woods. Ask a local railroad yard for obsolete railroad ties. Weathered wood may be found where old buildings have been wrecked; small pieces can be scrounged from forested areas and seashores.

Junk shops have many wooden objects that can be dismantled, cut up, and reused. Jacqueline Fogel uses only wood she has found from wrecked buildings and from discarded furniture.

DRYING AND SEALING

It has already been mentioned that logs tend to crack, or "check," as they dry. When the bark is removed, drying occurs at a more rapid rate, causing radial checks that begin in the sapwood and move into the heartwood. Such checks open and close, depending upon the humidity, even when the wood is hundreds of years old. (In our homes, doors that swell and stick in rainy weather are an example of such movement in wood.) Whether an artist wishes to use freshly cut or dried, cured wood is a matter of preference and availability.

Boards purchased from a lumberyard have been air- or kiln-dried, and only a small amount of moisture remains; therefore checking is not a major concern. Grades that have checks can be rejected. The sculptor who carves directly from logs finds that checking is his major technical problem. David Hostetler says: "I have tried many solutions. An early American wood-carver hollowed the wood, permitting air to circulate through the inside. When I carve a very green log I find that hollowing it really helps reduce the drying strains that result in checks. At the end of a day's carving I cover the log with heavy plastic to hold back the rapid drying that occurs when wood is brought indoors. An uncovered piece will check severely in a short time. Once the sculptor is finished, it is sealed and has a chance to adjust *slowly* to the drier interior environment, and checking is not so severe."

Many sculptors prefer to work only on logs that have cured two to four years. They cite the practice of early furniture and violin makers who stacked barns full of logs so that they would cure adequately for the next generation to use. When a log is left to cure, it should be placed off the ground so it won't rot. It will air-dry in a garage, basement, or outdoors.

What if checks occur despite curing, hollowing, sealing, and other precautions? Attitudes vary. Many sculptors advocate a philosophy of "truth of materials." If checks are in the nature of wood, they should be ignored. Others object to checks, and may fill them in with splinters of the wood or with wood filler.

There are several ways to seal a log to inhibit the rapid drying that causes severe checks. Freshly cut logs can be sealed with hot melted paraffin brushed on the cut surfaces. The log may be covered with heavy plastic to hold in the moisture. Commercial wood sealers are available. Only the cut ends and surfaces should be sealed; never the bark. Bark, nature's protective coating during growth, also protects the cut log from drying too rapidly.

Hollowing may not always be practical for the artist whose final form will have interior cuts. Once interior surfaces have been carved, they will have much the same effect as hollowing because the wood can dry from the inside out as well as the outside in. Checks seldom cause a block of wood to become so defective it falls in two: they don't destroy the wood structurally. A carver must recognize that radial checks appear in all logs and that they are a natural characteristic of wood.

Of all art media, wood probably is the most versatile. It can be cut, bent, burnished, polished, grooved, carved, split, joined, glued, nailed, pegged, scratched, pulped, petrified, pressured, shaped, and aged. Listening to lectures, reading about techniques, looking at things made of wood may stimulate you to approach the material in ways you hadn't thought about. But actually placing the wood on a saw, gouging it, burning it, and experimenting with it under many conditions is the most satisfying way to become familiar with its infinite variety.

WOOD SELECTION CHART

SPECIES	Comparative Weights[1]	Color[2]	Hand Tool Working	Nail Ability[3]	Relative Density	General Strength[4]	Resistance to Decay[5]	Wood Finishing[6]	Cost[7]
HARDWOODS[8]									
APITONG	Heavy	Reddish Brown	Hard	Poor	Medium	Good	High	Poor	Medium High
ASH, brown	Medium	Light Brown	Medium	Medium	Hard	Medium	Low	Medium	Medium
ASH, tough white	Heavy	Off-White	Hard	Poor	Hard	Good	Low	Medium	Medium
ASH, soft white	Medium	Off-White	Medium	Medium	Medium	Low	Low	Medium	Medium Low
AVODIRE	Medium	Golden Blond	Medium	Medium	Medium	Low	Low	Medium	High
BALSAWOOD	Light	Cream White	Easy	Good	Soft	Low	Low	Poor	Medium
BASSWOOD	Light	Cream White	Easy	Good	Soft	Low	Low	Medium	Medium
BEECH	Heavy	Light Brown	Hard	Poor	Hard	Good	Low	Easy	Medium
BIRCH	Heavy	Light Brown	Hard	Poor	Hard	Good	Low	Easy	High
BUTTERNUT	Light	Light Brown	Easy	Good	Soft	Low	Medium	Medium	Medium
CHERRY, black	Medium	Medium Reddish Brown	Hard	Poor	Hard	Good	Medium	Easy	High
CHESTNUT	Light	Light Brown	Medium	Medium	Medium	Medium	High	Poor	Medium
COTTONWOOD	Light	Greyish White	Medium	Good	Soft	Low	Low	Poor	Low
ELM, soft grey	Medium	Cream Tan	Hard	Good	Medium	Medium	Medium	Medium	Medium Low
GUM, red	Medium	Reddish Brown	Medium	Medium	Medium	Medium	Medium	Medium	Medium High
HICKORY, true	Heavy	Reddish Tan	Hard	Poor	Hard	Good	Low	Medium	Low
HOLLY	Medium	White to Grey	Medium	Medium	Hard	Medium	Low	Easy	Medium
KORINA	Medium	Pale Golden	Medium	Good	Medium	Medium	Low	Medium	High
MAGNOLIA	Medium	Yellowish Brown	Medium	Medium	Medium	Medium	Low	Easy	Medium
MAHOGANY, Honduras	Medium	Golden Brown	Easy	Good	Medium	Medium	High	Medium	High
MAHOGANY, Philippine	Medium	Medium Red	Easy	Good	Medium	Medium	High	Medium	Medium High
MAPLE, hard	Heavy	Reddish Cream	Hard	Poor	Hard	Good	Low	Easy	Medium High
MAPLE, soft	Medium	Reddish Brown	Hard	Poor	Hard	Good	Low	Easy	Medium Low
OAK, red (average)	Heavy	Flesh Brown	Hard	Medium	Hard	Good	Low	Medium	Medium
OAK, white (average)	Heavy	Greyish Brown	Hard	Medium	Hard	Good	High	Medium	Medium High
POPLAR, yellow	Medium	Light to Dark Yellow	Easy	Good	Soft	Low	Low	Easy	Medium
PRIMA VERA	Medium	Straw Tan	Medium	Medium	Medium	Medium	Medium	Medium	High
SYCAMORE	Medium	Flesh Brown	Hard	Good	Medium	Medium	Low	Easy	Medium Low
WALNUT, black	Heavy	Dark Brown	Medium	Medium	Hard	Good	High	Medium	High
WILLOW, black	Light	Medium Brown	Easy	Good	Soft	Low	Low	Medium	Medium Low
SOFTWOODS[9]									
CEDAR, Tennessee Red	Medium	Red	Medium	Poor	Medium	Medium	High	Easy	Medium
CYPRESS	Medium	Yellow to Reddish Brown	Medium	Good	Soft	Medium	High	Poor	Medium High
FIR, Douglas	Medium	Orange-Brown	Medium	Poor	Soft	Medium	Medium	Poor	Medium
FIR, white	Light	Nearly White	Medium	Poor	Soft	Low	Low	Poor	Low
PINE, yellow longleaf	Medium	Orange to Reddish Brown	Hard	Poor	Medium	Good	Medium	Medium	Medium
PINE, northern white (Pinus Strobus)	Light	Cream to Reddish Brown	Easy	Good	Soft	Low	Medium	Medium	Medium High
PINE, ponderosa	Light	Orange to Reddish Brown	Easy	Good	Soft	Low	Low	Medium	Medium
PINE, sugar	Light	Creamy Brown	Easy	Good	Soft	Low	Medium	Poor	Medium High
REDWOOD	Light	Deep Reddish Brown	Easy	Good	Soft	Medium	High	Poor	Medium
SPRUCES (average)	Light	Nearly White	Medium	Medium	Soft	Low	Low	Medium	Medium

[1]Kiln dried weight.
[2]Heartwood. Sap is whitish.
[3]Comparative splitting tendencies.
[4]Combined bending and compressive strength.
[5]No wood will decay unless exposed to moisture. Resistance to decay estimate refers to only heartwood.
[6]Ease of finishing with clear or "natural" finishes.
[7]Prices for best grade.
[8]Leaf bearing tree.
[9]Cone and needle bearing trees.

Courtesy, Frank Paxton Lumber Company, Chicago

TOOLS AND THEIR USES

The best tool to use for any job is the one that will produce the results you want. This may be anything from a penknife to an all-purpose power woodworking tool with attachments. Tools range from the simple saw and hammer in every home workshop to modern industrial power tools. (See Chapter 5 for special wood-carving tools.) When using tools, and especially power units, proper safety precautions must be rigidly enforced and respected. Generally these rules apply:

1. Do become familiar with the tool by reading directions and practicing on scrap lumber.

2. Don't allow yourself to become overconfident. The person who knows the safety rules and ignores them often gets hurt. Do remain a beginner where safety is concerned.

3. Don't wear clothes or articles that hang or dangle, such as long neckties, loose sleeves, rings, wristwatches, or anything that might get caught in the machinery or saw blade. Girls should keep long hair tied back with a ribbon or scarf.

4. Do keep hands in sight and clear of moving parts.

5. Never reach across a machine while it is running. Never try to stop a blade with your hand. Never pick a cutoff from the table

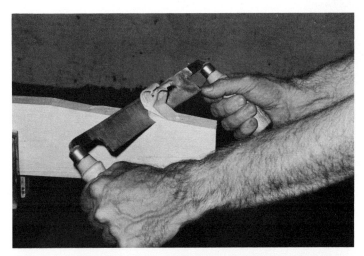

The drawknife enables you to shape a piece of wood more quickly than other hand tools do. It takes practice to master the correct position and quick, strong strokes.

Cutting wood across the grain is called "crosscutting," as shown here; cutting with the grain is "ripping."

With a chain saw a huge wooden log can be stripped and roughed out in minutes. The same job would take several days of hard labor with an ax.

When power tools are not available, the saw and ax are good standbys. Some artists like the slower development they achieve with hand tools.

while the blade is running; it may drop and swing the piece of wood at you.

6. Do switch off the machine and pull out the plug before you replace blades, drill bits, or other parts. Detach power when you are finished working with a machine so that others can't accidentally turn it on.

7. Keep tools sharp and clean. Sweep sawdust from floor frequently to prevent slipping on it.

8. Do wear safety glasses when engaged in any operation with hand or power tools that causes chips to fly.

9. Always *think* about what you are doing before you do it, and be sure every action you take is the safest!

Most readers will be familiar with tools in the home workshop such as coping saws, straight and crosscut saws, hand drills, hammers, pliers, and planes. These may be examined in any hardware store. They are easy and relatively safe to use. Demonstrations on the use of power tools specifically for wood sculptures follow.

David Hostetler works on an elm log for one of his "American Wife" series. Hostetler uses a chain saw and ax to bring a log to workable size, then hollows the log with an old-time barn drill. He meticulously shapes with mallet and gouges and chisels.

Photo, Jon Webb

TABLE-SAW SCULPTURES

Once you learn the mechanics of tools and the safety rules for using them, you will be amazed at the artistic results you can achieve by creatively cutting wood. Students at Chicago's Institute of Design, at the Illinois Institute of Technology, produce fascinating sculptures during the first or second sessions in basic design workshop classes. Instructor Ray Pearson emphasizes that tools are simply tools; they are not a substitute for creativity. But using tools and thinking creatively is a forceful combination.

Attempting to create sculptures with power tools will acquaint you with the potentials and limitations of the machine. What is more important is that the beginner learns to perceive all sorts of possible shapes within a simple piece of wood. As cuts are made around a block of wood, two or more faces of the wood are being cut into simultaneously.

When you place a piece of wood on a table saw, don't try to copy the examples shown; see how original your own piece of sculpture can be. In the beginning a sense of order and discipline in developing the cuts is essential. Later, you can vary size and distances of cuts and shapes. Use any kind of wood available in 2" × 2", 1" × 2", dowels, clothes rods, and so on.

Begin by setting the blade of your table saw low, and slide a block along with the saw guide. Make several cuts at regular intervals. Then angle the blade and raise it slightly until you are able to make another cut to meet the first, and remove a wedge of wood. In this way you can make all kinds of angular cuts. By overlapping cuts on different sides of the block, you'll sculpture the wood into unique effects.

Other novel patterns can be achieved by making numerous cuts in a length of clothes rod. Experiment by changing the angle and height of your blade and also by turning the fence guide so that you feed the wood into the blade at different angles.

Study the examples to determine the variety of cuts that were made to achieve the effect. Then try to make your own unusual table-saw sculptures.

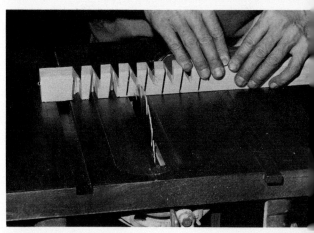

Table-saw sculptures are not meant to be functional; they are a lesson in the use of the saw and in creativity. Usually, one can't visualize the finished sculpture until the pattern begins to evolve under the cuts. Each result is unique. They are particularly exciting when they emerge after a student has just learned how to use the saw.

All examples are from Ray Pearson's classes, Institute of Design, I.I.T., Chicago. Photos, author

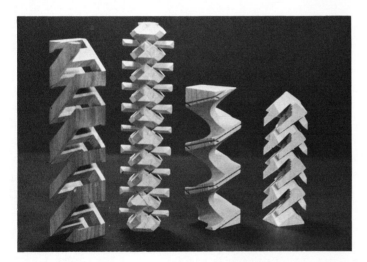

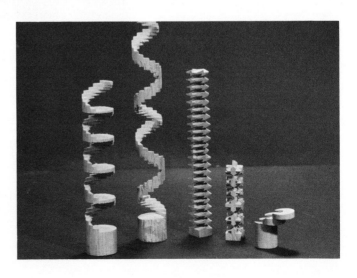

LATHE SCULPTURES

If you think of a lathe as only a tool for making decorative spindles for chair legs or for turning round shapes, think again. You can make turnings to create shapes as beautiful and graceful as these. The trick is "off-center" turning.

First become familiar with how the lathe works normally by centering a block of wood on the lathe and making shapes—any shapes —with lathe chisels. Because very soft woods tend to splinter, select a fairly hard wood. Do not use wood with defects such as checks or knots. Once you have a fairly competent turning, remove the work and replace it on the lathe *off-center*. This can be done in several ways. You can recenter one end at a slightly different point; you can recenter both ends at different points; you can cut two new parallel faces at an angle in the original face, and re-center the block on these faces. Then simply turn another pattern on top of the first one.

When you work off-center, the wood may jiggle against the carving chisel. Hold the chisel securely until you get the feel. Stop often and check the work. The results are usually odd and graceful. Often, beautiful patterns emerge in woods that are heavily grained and figured. You can also sand the objects more easily while they are on the lathe by simply letting the lathe turn and holding the sanding material against the wood.

The lathe is also used for turning bowls, candlesticks, and other accessories.

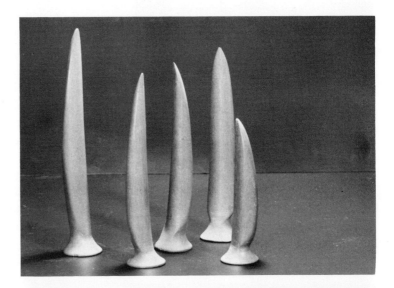

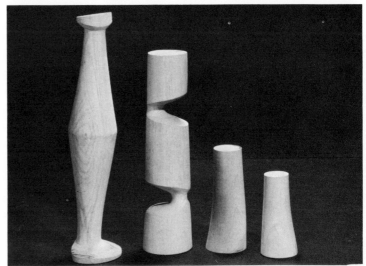

*All lathe sculpture ex-
amples are from Ray Pear-
son's classes, Institute of
Design, I.I.T., Chicago.
Photos, author*

Stretching wood with jigsaw cuts.

Student, University of Illinois at the Chicago Circle. Photo, John Walley

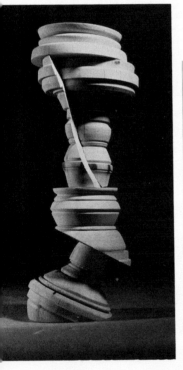

Student, Institute of Design, I.I.T., Chicago. Photo, author

SCULPTURES WITH JIGSAWS AND BAND SAWS

A band saw and a jigsaw can be used for endless artistic projects. These tools are easily mastered by women, too, who may not feel so comfortable with the large, open revolving blade of a table saw. Women, particularly, are delighted to discover that these tools, usually considered only in the domain of carpentry, can also be used to turn out unusual artistic objects.

The jigsaw, shown in use, can cut curves and intricate patterns, and make inside cuts and fancy scrolls. Its blade is ideal for cutting fine, tiny pieces of wood used for inlay, for building up patterns, and even for stretching wood by notching it. The stretched piece shown can be duplicated many times, arranged on a backing, and painted to become an intricate relief pattern. You can actually do some basic carving with this tool, and, if you like, finish with hand-carving.

The band saw has a heavier blade than the jigsaw, and is used for heavier cutting procedures. It may be used for fragmenting (see page 6) by cutting apart recognizable objects and reassembling them into new relationships. It is indispensable for cutting up small pieces of wood used in assemblage. The table of the saw may be tilted to produce angle cuts, or the piece itself may be held on an angle. However, if angle cuts on two pieces are to be glued together, their angled edges must be perfectly matched; therefore the tilted table with a guide that feeds the block through the blade is best.

First become familiar with the potentials of each power tool. Once you know what the tool can do, design for the sake of design, and not for the tool. If the ultimate design cannot be done with a tool with which you are familiar, then find the tool that can do the job or do it by hand. Don't let the tool dictate design once you have decided on the form a sculpture is to take.

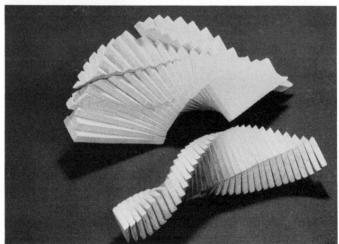

Sculptures and fragmented forms
made by cutting and regluing.
*Students of Ray Pearson, Institute
of Design, I.I.T., Chicago. Photos,
author*

Floor-model drill press.

Fly cutter attachment is used for making large holes.

DRILL-PRESS SCULPTURES

Drill patterns of holes to create striking effects. Begin with a piece of ¾″ board or a 2″ × 2″, and drill holes partway through in some areas and all the way through in others. Turn the wood from back to front; drill out corners. Use bits of different sizes for holes of varying sizes. Overlap circles and combine various patterns for results that will be continually surprising and attractive.

You can also cut a core out of a 2″ × 2″ or a square block without drilling into either end. The secret is to drill pattern holes along each face, making sure the holes on one face overlap those on another. The core is carved out of the block by the drill without going down through the center, as shown in the photograph at right.

The drill press is particularly important for doweling and pegging wood constructions by a technique shown in Chapter 4. Several attachments are available for a drill press. Many can be ingeniously used for creatively designed sculptures. Try such things as the fly cutter, the counterbore, the dovetail cutter.

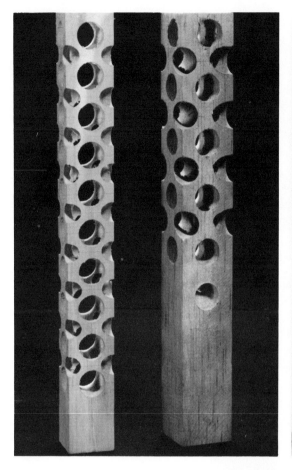

Drill-press sculptures.
*Students of Ray Pearson, Institute
of Design, I.I.T., Chicago.
Photos, author*

This portable, lightweight Moto Shop is a boon to artists. It can be set on a kitchen table, yet it has ample working capacity for sawing, sanding, carving, routing, and grinding.

Courtesy, Dremel Mfg. Co., Racine, Wisconsin

Portable power, jig, and saber saws are versatile. They can be used for notching, cutouts, ripping, crosscutting, mitering, and beveling. Heavy-duty models can cut logs and beams.

Courtesy, Skil Corporation

PORTABLE POWER TOOLS

Portable power tools are versatile, and as useful for the artist as they are for the crafts-man and carpenter. Though they lack some of the precision and convenience of floor units, familiarity and experimentation with the tools will enable you to make a variety of sculptures.

The tools shown are only a few of the types of portable saws, drills, and sanders; compared to floor models, they are inexpensive. With attachments, they can be used for myriad woodworking operations. If you are unsure of the best tool for your work, many stores have rental units available. It's unwise to buy a band saw, for example, if a jigsaw would serve your needs better. Rent one or both to determine which you prefer; then buy.

It is difficult to cut very small pieces of wood with portable saws because the wood must be clamped. Clamping small, oddly shaped pieces of driftwood, for instance, and trying to saw into smaller pieces, is almost impossible. It is possible to mount portable saws on small worktables to make them stationary enough to feed work into, but this is not so satisfactory as table equipment.

Certain safety measures are essential in working with portable tools. Always be familiar with what your unit can and cannot do. Do not try to use it for procedures for which it was not intended. To force work or rush wood through saw blades may cause a blade to snap, with dire consequences. Always keep the power cord away from the blade of the tool.

When replacing blades, bits, or attachments, always remove the cord from the outlet plug.

Always keep tools clean and in optimum working condition by following instructions for oiling, changing brushes, and so on.

Always work where light is sufficient. Do not wear clothes that hang loosely or articles that might become entangled in the saw or drill.

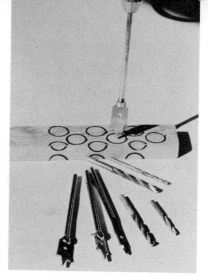

Portable electric drills can be used to make cutouts similar to those accomplished with a drill press. Bits are available for large and small holes.

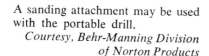

A sanding attachment may be used with the portable drill.
Courtesy, Behr-Manning Division of Norton Products

A portable electric sander is a boon to many artists; depending upon the type of finish one wants, it can be a time-saving adjunct.
Courtesy, Behr-Manning Division of Norton Products

A floor-model belt sander.

LA PRIMA DOÑA. Jacqueline Fogel. An old radio cabinet becomes the support for this songstress created from found pieces of posts and furniture parts. Old wood is stripped of its original finish, then carved, assembled, and repainted with artist's oil paints.

Courtesy, Krasner Gallery, New York. Photo, Rupert Finegold

chapter 3

Painting and Finishing Wood

The cellular structure of wood requires surface treatment to protect it from dust and deterioration. Transparent and opaque finishes are used, depending upon the effect desired and the quality and color of the wood.

Fifteenth- and sixteenth-century wood carvings were almost always polychromed as protection and also because artisans felt that color was an important aspect of the image. Restorers often report that when paint has peeled away from such carvings, much of the wood is still in good condition. In other instances the paint has served as a shell that, once broken, has permitted the wood beneath the paint to suffer decay by time or insects.

The Forest Products Laboratory of the United States Department of Agriculture continually conducts experiments seeking better and more lasting coatings for wood. Much of their accumulated knowledge has been incorporated into the chemical makeup of paints and finishes.

Attitudes toward the use of color on sculpture varies. A modern taste for uncolored sculpture found theoretical support in the mystique of "truth to materials," and also in an artistic discipline aimed at "purity"—the idea that a sculpture should be composed of one set of elements only.

A shift to color in sculpture occurred gradually. Picasso, Archipenko, and Laurens made colored sculptures. Nadelman began to use color around 1917. By the 1930's more colored sculpture emerged. Alexander Calder's first showing of brightly colored mobiles sparked the use of color, and in the last ten years, colored sculptures have bloomed like flowers in a summer garden.

The reasons the artist uses color are diverse. One reason is to imitate naturalism, as in the painting of a sculpture of a human figure. Probably the most evident use is for a stylized realism where color is applied in non-naturalistic ways that combine the effect of color and sculpture as one. The result is an inventiveness that is far more expressive and appealing than imitation of the natural. Such painted sculptures use color to describe an abstract concept, to be decorative or symbolic.

Color is applied to nonrepresentational sculpture to unify forms and planes and to elevate them to an invented logic. Often, color will define volume and mass, demarcating forms already indicated in the sculpture.

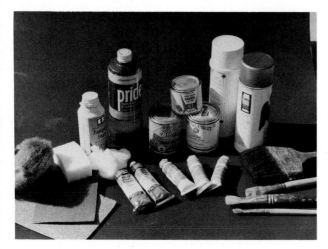

Oil paints, acrylic paints, stains, varnishes, waxes, and antique effects are all applicable to wood sculptures.

Color can develop forms where none are indicated in the modeling. Details such as a hand, facial features, or clothing are painted upon continuous unaccented form, as in the sculptures of women by David Hostetler. Louise Nevelson uses monotone color to unify the parts of a sculpture. Anne Arnold uses wood of varying grains that detract from the form, and then applies color to bring all the parts together.

Color is also cleverly used to distort form, to create prominences where none exist, and to suppress those that do. It can also create optical illusions. Painted design on a construction can make a plane appear entirely different from what it really is. The artist uses color to create a mood or to designate humor or pathos. Marisol uses color and drawing to show personalities and their emotions.

COLORING

Wood requires certain basic treatments for specific color applications. Because wood is porous, it must be sealed to prevent paint from seeping into the surface. A clear wood sealer, such as shellac, varnish, or acrylic, may be applied as a base coat. An opaque primer may also be used to seal and to provide a base color. The final color surface is applied by using any of a variety of commercial products. Paint coatings may be protected by artist's glazes in matte and gloss. Whenever different paint products are used in several coatings,

check to make sure the products are compatible. For example, if lacquer is used over enamel, the enamel will craze and peel because the products are not compatible.

A range of easily available paint products includes:
• Artist's oil paints used full strength or thinned with turpentine.
• Household paints in gloss and flat finishes.
• Sign painter's paint in cans.
• Latex and acrylic paints.
• Acrylic and plastic base coatings in matte and gloss finishes that may be brushed or sprayed over painted surfaces.

TRANSPARENT FINISHES

To stain wood is to apply a material that permeates the pores of the wood and changes the color without altering the grain or patterns. Walnut stain can be applied on pine or plywood to simulate the color of natural walnut. Aerosol foam and liquid stains offer great flexibility of application. Always stain raw wood; then seal it with varnish, shellac, acrylic sprays, or epoxy resins. Wax over stain acts as a preservative. Open-grain woods may be treated with a coating of wood filler before sealing.

Stains may also be made by thinning artist's oil paints with turpentine until they are fluid enough to be brushed or rubbed into the wood's surface and so penetrate the pores.

INKS, DYES, AND DRAWING

Clothing dyes, aniline dye, colored inks, and direct drawing with pencil, felt tip pen, and so on, are among the many surface color treatments shown in the following pages. These materials may be applied to sealed and unsealed wood.

The expressive and imaginative quality of a ceremonial board from the Papuan Gulf of New Guinea illustrates the high degree of two-dimensional design on wood used by the Melanesians.

Courtesy, Art Institute of Chicago

Primitive carved and painted wooden rattle from British Columbia is a combination of painted and natural wood surface.

Courtesy, Smithsonian Institution, Washington, D. C.

Removing old stains or lightening dark woods can be done with liquid bleach preparations and sponge. Wear rubber gloves for protection.

Dents in a piece of wood can be raised by placing a moist cloth over the bare wood and applying a hot iron over the cloth. You may have to repeat this two or three times.

ICON. Victor Four. Surface painting and staining on weathered wood gives an antique effect, as though the piece were centuries old.

Courtesy, Lefebre Gallery, New York

WAXING AND OILING

When no paints or stains are used, a surface treatment with wax, shellac, or Danish oils may be applied as a preservative. Al Vrana, who works in southern Florida, applies a furniture paste wax mixed with mineral spirits and insecticides because of the termite problem. Over a week's time he brushes on five or six coats until the wood has a deep penetrating protection that also brings out the grain. Chaim Gross applies a coating of shellac mixed with alcohol to prevent dirt and dust from penetrating the wood.

REMOVING COLOR, AND BLEACHING

An artist may find a piece of painted wood that he wishes to reuse. If he can't paint over the color, he will have to strip the wood down to its natural surface. Many commercial paint removers are available in hardware stores. If some traces of paint remain after paint remover has been used, they may be eliminated by sanding or by gently passing a blowtorch over the surface; this burns away paint pigments and oils.

Fascinating effects may be achieved by bleaching a nondescript piece of wood. Wood bleach, also available in hardware stores, comes in two solutions. With some bleaches you mix the two together; with others you put one on and wait a half hour or so before putting on the other. An acid solution pulls the color out of the wood; the other solution neutralizes the acid so it won't continue to eat into the wood.

Bleach actually makes wood become snow-white, almost like plaster. Dark-brown walnut and mahogany will bleach snow-white. Though the color is gone, the grains remain. After a piece is bleached it can be sanded, waxed, stained with any color, and sealed. Transparent colors appear much more transparent. If bleached wood is left in the bright

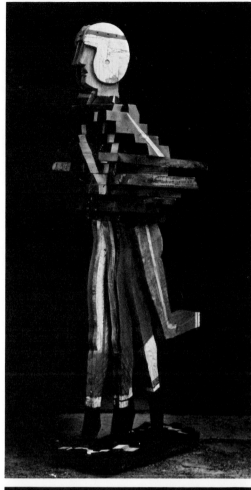

THE ALL-AMERICAN. Sidney Simon. 1956. 6′ high. Assorted woods partially painted. Texture varies from rough to smooth.

Courtesy, artist

sun, the pigment from deep inside the wood will eventually recolor the surface. But experimentation with bleach on wood can result in unusual surface colors.

SMOOTHING

After painting a sculpture, some smoothing is necessary. There are various kinds of smoothing materials, depending upon the final result desired. Books devoted to the finishing of woods are available, and these should be referred to. For other information write to paint companies that sell abrasives. Sandpaper is made in several degrees of roughness and types of grit. You can better understand the differences by handling them and comparing them at your hardware-store counter. For hand-sanding, place the paper on a block of wood, working first with a rough, then with a finer sandpaper.

Once you apply a finish to wood, the result is not permanent if you change your mind. Paint can be removed; stains can be lifted out. Forman Onderdonk made a sculpture from which he has removed the paint color four times until presently it possesses its natural wood tone.

As you observe wood, learn to identify the various ways in which the surfaces were finished. Think of the compatibility between the type of wood, its texture, the technique used, and the finish. Ask yourself if the finish detracted from or enhanced the surface or if some other finish might have done the job better. These are decisions you will have to make as you create art with wood.

KING OF CLUBS. Leo Jenson. Painted plywood.

Courtesy, United States Plywood Corporation, New York

STONES. Herbert Sandmann. Pieces of 2″ × 4″ cut, filed, burned, glued, then painted with tempera color, and waxed.
Courtesy, artist

WHITE RELIEF. Eduardo Ramírez. 1966. Relief structure painted white is meant to capture ever-changing shadows for interest.
Courtesy, Graham Gallery, New York.
Photo, Nathan Rabin

LA APARICIÓN. Antonio López-García. 1964. When wood is carved and completely painted, the type and grade of wood used are unimportant.

Courtesy, Galería Juana Mordó, Madrid.

Photo, R. Domache

MIMI. Chaim Gross. 1954. Lignum vitae wood. 15″ high. Form and wood texture are interdependent. A coat of shellac thinned with alcohol is applied only for protection.

Courtesy, artist. Photo, Soichi Sunami

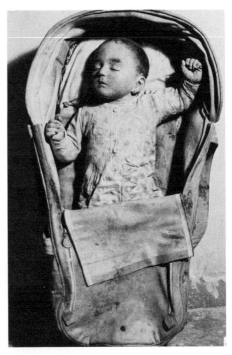

MARÍA DURMIENDO. Antonio López-García. 1964. Completely carved of wood, and painted.

Courtesy, Galería Juana Mordó, Madrid

SERIES # 2–9. Ralph White. 1962. Mesquite wood. 5′ 9″ high. Orange-enameled surface has a smooth high-gloss finish.

Photo, Scott Hyde

SLEEPING BLACK NUDE. Anne Arnold. 1966. Pine. 16″ high, 32″ wide, 83″ long. Large pieces of Maine pine are lightweight, easy to handle, and free of knots. However, the pine sheets have color variations that disturb the finished form. Painting, the sculptor believes, makes the piece more visible as a total unit with shifting planes.
Courtesy, Sculptors Guild, Inc., New York.
Photo, Rudolph Burckhardt

DANCER. John W. Kearney. 1966. 8′ high. Flat paint with textured carved surface.

Courtesy, artist

ALP: FENCE. James Russell. 1966. 66″ wide, 64″ high, 5″ deep. Wood is used as a surface and as constructed parts for paint and collage. Russell's constructions have literary content, in this case, numbers and rainbow-painted balls have James Joyce symbolism.

Courtesy, Ruth White Gallery, New York

EACH IN HIS OWN WAY. Natalie Cole. Stained plywood figures on a painted surface.

Courtesy, Ontario East Gallery, Chicago

COVENTRY. Gabriel Kohn. 1962. 32″ × 40″. Laminated parts pegged together give the artist liberty to improvise fresh relationships of form.
Courtesy, Marlborough-Gerson Gallery, New York.
Photo, Rudolph Burckhardt

chapter 4

Laminating, Joining, Pegging

As the sculptor conceived forms more expansive than that of a single cylindrical log, he sought methods for joining pieces of wood. Joints had to be permanent and strong. They could not detract from the esthetic quality of the work. Until the middle of the 1700's, when adhesives came into use, all woodwork was dry-jointed. Today gluing is often combined with joints made by nailing, screwing, bolting, pegging, and other carpentering techniques. Relief constructions are mainly dependent upon glue to hold the parts to a backing.

GLUING AND LAMINATING

When a sculptor envisions a large, monumental work, he may require a mass of wood larger than a log or dressed board. Modern glue compounds have made the task of joining woods easy, versatile, permanent, and satisfactory. Many of today's sculptures involve laminating and/or gluing several boards together.

Plywood is the prime example of laminated board. Thin layers of wood are peeled from around a tree much as paper is pulled from a roll. Three to five layers are laminated, each layer at cross grain to the other, for extra strength. With such large laminated sheets the artist can expand forms architecturally. By laminating boards he can combine more than one kind of wood in a sculpture. He has the opportunity to juxtapose grain relationships in different directions.

Any of the surfaces of cut board may be glued: the faces, edges, ends, or all three. Joints will strengthen the glue, and vice versa, though for some laminations only glue may be used. When warped and uneven boards are glued, pockets may result that eventually cause the jointed surfaces to separate. Boards that are cross-grain laminated should not be used outdoors; the different movement from expansion causes cross-grain woods to separate at the glue joints. Choose select boards, quartersawed to minimize warpage, for laminated sculptures.

Wood, because of its cellular structure, can be glued very easily and rapidly. Generally, the lighter the weight of the wood, the more easily it will glue. Glue fills the pores of the wood; it does not penetrate the cell walls. Some artists maintain that the older glues tend to fall apart in time, but today's glues are so strong that if a piece is under strain, the wood may break and the joined portion remain intact.

White emulsion glues such as casein and acrylic resin are most popular for wood that is to be kept indoors. They dry clear and are very strong, but they are not waterproof. If color is desired around a glue line, these water-base emulsion glues may be tinted with acrylic

CUTTING BOARD. Junior High student. Remnants of varying woods are end- and edge-glued. *Skiles Junior High School, Evanston, Illinois*

CHECKERBOARD. Gerald J Tomany. Square of mahogany and butternut. Zebrawood ends have been glued to a backboard. Edges of each square had to be glued also.

CYLINDER. Fred Borcherdt. Maple and walnut rounds cut on a band saw, and laminated.

CONSTRUCTION. Fred Borcherdt. Scrap pieces of wood shaped with a band saw, glued, and fitted together like intricate parts of a puzzle. Base made by laminating rectangles of wood, shaping and sanding.

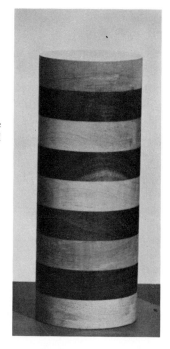

paints. Casein glue is especially good for bonding oily woods such as teak and pitch pine. It can be mixed with sawdust to form a wood putty that will match the color and texture of the wood.

Waterproof glue should be used on sculptures to be placed outdoors. This usually applies to redwood and painted wood projects. Epoxy resin or resorcin resin glues are so dependable underwater that they are used for boat hulls. Contact cement can be used when gluing wood to metal, plastics, stone, and nonporous materials.

Epoxy resin can be built up to greater thicknesses than casein or acrylic glues, an advantage when boards are warped or do not fit well together. Epoxies come in two solutions that must be mixed. They are available at hardware stores in twin tubes. In large quantities, they are usually available only from industrial firms, which frequently neglect to put directions on labels of gallon cans. You'll have to experiment with scrap boards until you find the best mixture for your purpose. Some epoxies are also pigmented, and tend to leave a dark glue line that may or may not be objectionable.

For small bonding projects, a thermo-grip electric gun applies a line of hot glue that bonds and dries in sixty seconds. Wood can be sawed, nailed, and carved immediately. Larger glue guns, now used by the furniture manufacturers, are a boon for multiple lamination projects. They are expensive, but they eliminate slippage of boards and drying time. Bonding and drying are immediate.

There are two opposing philosophies about craftsmanship in sculpture. The fastidi-ous, carpenter-minded craftsman believes in perfect joints carefully prepared, glued, and smoothed. The opposing philosophy, termed anticraftsmanship, is aimed at breaking down tradition. In rebellion, the anticraftsman may use wood haphazardly, permit dowels to protrude that are splintered and uneven, and allow glue to drip and run at imperfectly formed joints. He may consider his technique to be an expression of difference in purpose and in end results desired. Neat, clean, precise technique may express precise ideas; a flowing, loose technique projects a plastic idea. Above all, form is the important consideration, apart from the manner in which the sculpture is constructed.

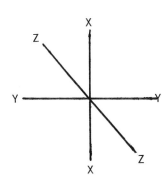

To laminate, be sure boards are planed accurately. (Always measure twice and cut once.) Maple, oak, and poplar boards are cut to size accurately and placed in various directions. Check to see that boards are of almost exact thickness. If boards differ by even 1/32 of an inch, the differentials add up. Warped areas create voids between boards. Glue may fill the voids, but the joint tends to be weak. Boards may be set in three directions on an X-Y-Z axis.

Glue should be mixed according to directions. Sprinkle sawdust on newspapers spread on the floor. Sawdust catches dripping glue and makes cleaning up easier. Be sure all glue particles are thoroughly saturated or glue will not be efficient. Try to mix one batch for the entire job.

Glue is applied to flat surfaces and edges that are to adhere. Set boards on pieces of scrap lumber so they won't glue to paper.

When all boards have been spread with glue, carefully align them. They are slippery at this point. Some people recommend only enough glue to cover the surfaces. Tomany prefers to use more than enough glue, and let it ooze to be sure every portion of the board has glue on it. Sheets of clear or colored plastic may also be placed within a structure for a transparent or colored tone. Be sure to use the proper glue for various materials.

Put a weight (limestone is used here) on the horizontal boards first. Because bonding occurs quickly, boards must be in the correct positions. Place clamps where they are needed for the vertical joints. Follow the glue directions for drying time. When the laminated piece is dry, it is ready to be shaped.

Tools used for carving a laminated piece are a hatchet, gouge and mallet, rasps, and sharpening stones. When you are chipping the wood, wear safety glasses to prevent pieces from hitting your eyes.

Set the laminate on a block, and use a hatchet to develop the major shape.

Continue to work with mallet and gouge, chisels and rasps until the final form is reached. Always keep the tools sharp. (See Chapter 5, page 94, for sharpening techniques.) Smooth and finish as desired.

UNTITLED. Gerald J Tomany. 1967.
Red oak and poplar. 19″ high.
Photo, author

Tomany's pieces are smooth and beautifully re-
fined to a surface that has tactile, sensuous
qualities. The forms are based on organic shapes
observed in stones, roots, broken pieces of wood,
and so on. He may use a Danish oil or epoxy
wood sealer to finish.

UNTITLED. Gerald J Tomany. 1967.
Red oak, poplar, and beachwood.
23″ high.
Photo, author

UNTITLED. Gerald J Tomany. 1967. Zebrawood. 63″ high, including the base. By laminating highly figured zebrawood in different directions, an intricate, but carefully controlled, pattern becomes beautifully integrated with the simple form. Zebrawood is heavy and hard, and may be polished to a high luster.

Rear view.

Photos, author

EDGE AND END GLUING

Boards to be edge-glued should be put through a jointer to square all edges. Uneven edges prevent the glue line from becoming uniformly thick, and a weak joint will result.

Arrange the boards in a clamp, placing the buffer pieces at the ends to prevent the clamp from denting pieces that will become part of the sculpture.

Take the boards out one at a time and apply glue to each piece to be joined. White emulsion glues are commonly used for this work. Tighten the clamps for recommended drying time; then loosen the clamps just enough to relax the tension. Allow the piece to dry overnight.

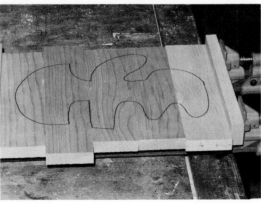

When the piece is dry, draw the pattern on the wood, and cut it with the jigsaw or band saw.

Uneven lengths and variable widths of redwood have been end- and edge-glued. By using heartwood and sapwood, different grains are combined for greater interest and beauty.

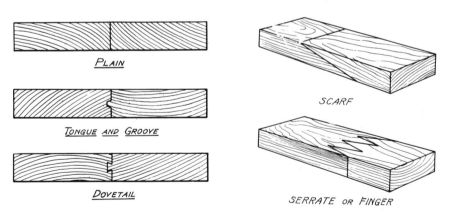

PLAIN

TONGUE AND GROOVE

DOVETAIL

SCARF

SERRATE OR FINGER

Butting and gluing edges do not result in so strong a joint as do edges that are reinforced with carpentry methods. The scarf makes a simple, strong joint. The finger, or serrated, joint is still stronger. Tongue-and-grove and dovetail joints are used with edge-gluing, and are particularly good where seasonal expansion and contraction of woods are factors. The type of joint must be determined by the wood used and the strength required for the final piece.

When you use screws that must be hidden in the structure, you can use on a drill press a system of bits which include a counterbore and a matching plug cutter. The counterbore drills a hole in the piece to be attached. This prepares a proper seating for the screw threads, shank, and flat head. The screw can be dropped below the surface up to a half-inch deep.

COUNTERSINKING AND PLUGGING

In many wood constructions it is essential to join the pieces of wood with screws, yet the screwheads are not usually compatible with the wood surface. The technique is to sink the screw below the surface of the wood and fill the hole with a peg made of the same wood or a different wood, depending upon the desired effect. Plugs can be made of the same wood as the sculpture; the grain may then be matched and the piece finished so the plug is barely discernible. Sometimes, however, the pegs are used as a decorative element, and are carefully placed on the sculptured surface.

The plug cutter produces a plug that fits the hole exactly. In placing the plug, arrange its grain to follow the grain of the main piece.

When the plug is cut, simply free it from the hole by prying it up gently with a screwdriver. This illustration shows a countersunk hole, a screw, a plug, and a plug already sunk to camouflage the screw. After sanding, the plug will barely show.

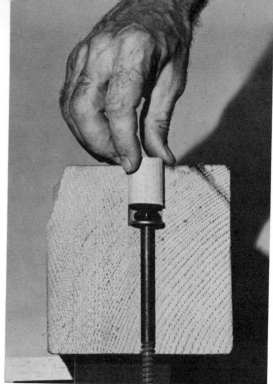

To join large pieces of timber, use this technique shown in cross section. Drill a hole in the top of one piece of wood large enough to accommodate a socket wrench. Sink a lag screw, placing a washer under the head. Tighten with with the socket wrench.

Then add a dowel over the head of the bolt in the same way the peg was used to camouflage a screw. Sand, or allow to protrude, as desired.

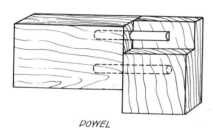

DOWEL

Doweling is a method for connecting and strengthening pieces of wood. Holes are drilled in each piece to be joined. The dowel, a cylindrical wooden rod, is placed so that it bridges the two pieces. For stationary joints the dowels are glued. For joints that are to move, as in kinetic sculpture, they can perform the function of an axle. Dowels may be purchased from ⅛″ to 1¼″ in diameter. Up to 1″ diameter the standard length is 3′; dowels 1¼″ in diameter are 4′. Dowels are cut along the grain, and will not match the wood being used in color or grain. An actual design results from the strategic placement of dowels, and must be accounted for in the final piece as an esthetic as well as a structural device.

Big Mama II. Forman Onderdonk. Painted wood. 5′ high. Laminated and doweled.

Photo, author

Wizard Willow. Forman Onderdonk. 6′ high. Large pieces of timber bolted, pegged, and glued. Pegs are esthetic and functional.

Collection, Joe Nathan, Glencoe, Illinois. Photo, author

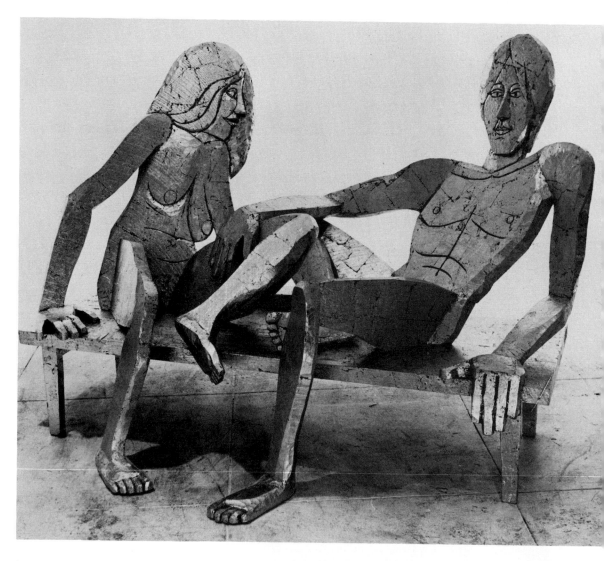

SEATED COUPLE. Anne Arnold. 1966.
White pine, gold-leafed. 58″ high, 78″
long, 50″ deep. Assembling broad pieces
of shaped wood permits expansion into
space in many ways. For these figures it
is necessary to develop compound joints
and attach the wood at odd angles. In the
photograph at right, taken during the construction stage, you can see how the
dowels are driven in. Additional carving
and sanding give a deep, rounded, three-
dimensional feeling to the flat boards.

Courtesy, Fischbach Gallery, New York.
Photo, Rudolph Burckhardt

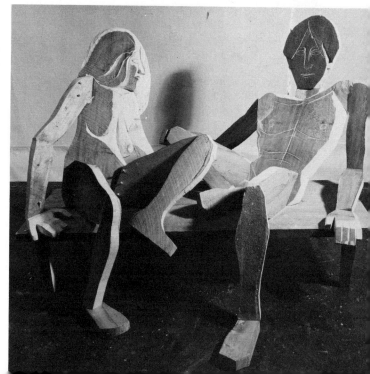

OTHER METHODS
OF JOINING WOOD

Many types of joining techniques may be required in one piece of sculpture. In this unpainted form Forman Onderdonk has used corrugated fasteners, nails, laminations, and dowels.

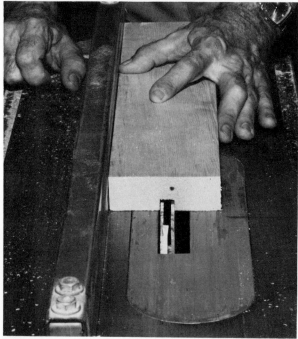

Grooving one piece of wood and setting another piece of wood into the groove creates a stronger joint than butting two pieces together. Grooves can be made with the dado cutter of a table saw. Set the blade of the dado the same distance apart as the thickness of the piece of wood to be inserted in the groove.

Grooved dado joint.

Another technique is the intersecting joint that can be made with a table saw, band saw, or handsaw.

Corrugated fasteners will strengthen edge-glued joints. Hammer them in on angles for greater strength.

Other types of joints.

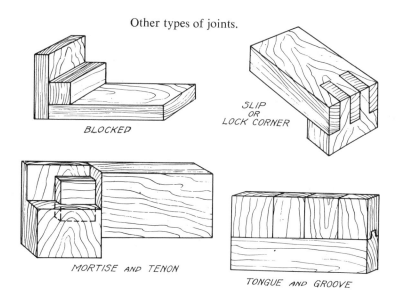

BLOCKED

SLIP
OR
LOCK CORNER

MORTISE AND TENON

TONGUE AND GROOVE

THE C.P.A. Sidney Simon. 1966. Black walnut, birch, and old wooden typeface. 6′ high. Planks of different sizes of two very different colored woods have been laminated; the pieces of type were glued. In the sideview photograph note that pegs have been added to join the laminated portions to the central block of wood. Woods are sanded and finished with only a few coats of wax.

THE C.P.A. (side view).

Photos, artist

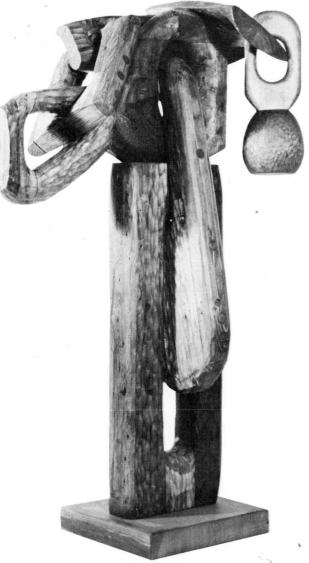

GROOM. William P. Sildar. 1966. 20″
× 42″. Wood carved, laminated, pegged,
and assembled.
Courtesy, Sculptors Guild, Inc.,
New York

MAINE TORSO. Mike Nevelson. 1962. Maine pine
wood on steel base. 5′ high, excluding base.
Courtesy, Wadsworth Atheneum,
Hartford, Connecticut.
Photo, E. Irving Blomstrann

T with Yellow and Blue. Hugh Townley. 1955.
16½" × 30".
Collection, Mr. and Mrs. Arnold Maremont,
Winnetka, Illinois

In these examples, dowels are used in several ways; they are functional, holding pieces of wood together; they are used as an axis on which other wood forms turn or move; they are carefully integrated into the design in a repeat motif. In Townley's example, the pegs are different sizes, and repeat the positive circular shape of the negative spaces. Anderson uses the same technique at the top of the carillon handles. To hold the crosspost, the dowels are structural but carefully balanced to give a repeat visual note. The dowels and pegs are deliberately darker to add to the design.

CARILLON II. John Anderson. 1963. 8⅝" high, 3⅝" wide, 1¾" deep.
Courtesy, Allan Stone Galleries, Inc., New York

BEL WEIR II. Sondra Beal. 1965. 48″ × 35″ × 28″. Wood carved, laminated, pegged, and assembled with motors for moving parts. Flat planes are painted. Some portions are directly carved; some are smoothed and others are painted. Combining techniques, finishes, and colors utilizes the natural qualities of woods, yet makes the entire sculpture dependent on the final form and artistic statement rather than on the materials. The imagery of mechanical forms is a popular theme of the contemporary artist working in wood or in metal.
Courtesy, B. C. Holland Gallery, Chicago. Photo, Nathan Rabin

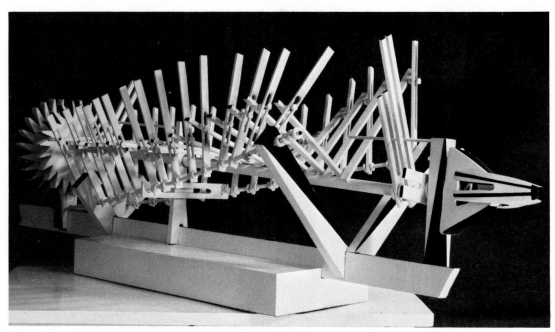

FISH. Audrey Skaling. 1967. Painted wood with all hand-carved pieces that undulate like a poetic articulation. 48″ × 35″ × 28″. The dowels become functional mechanistic axles rather than permanent joints. Miss Skaling's sculpture is a serious pun on mechanized society: it is a machine that does nothing.

Courtesy, Ruth White Gallery, New York. Photo, Walter Rosenblum

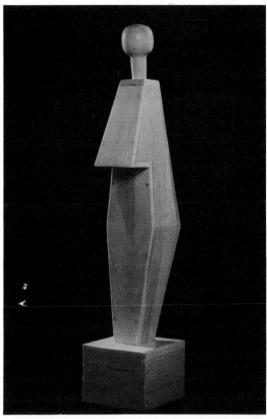

CHALET FIGURE. Mike Nevelson. 42″ high. Pine.
Photo, artist

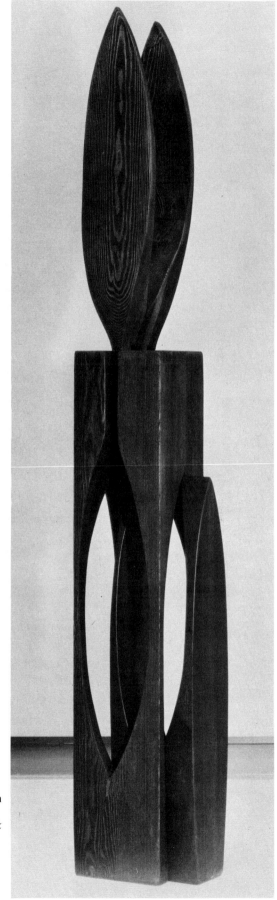

TRYST #2. Doris Chase. 1966. Laminated wood with
ebony stain. 102″ high.
Courtesy, Ruth White Gallery, New York

INSCRIBED FIGURE. Ynez Johnston. 1962.
Painted wood. 33″ high. The joints are
purposely left rough, as the artist tends
to fuse animal, bird, human, and architectural forms. Roughly jointed works
often earn the creators the title of "anti-
craftsmen." This does not mean the artists
are poor craftsmen or do not make good
use of their materials, it simply means
that sleek craftsmanship may represent
another form of expression.
Courtesy, Adele Bednarz Galleries,
Los Angeles

MORATORIUM. William Dubin.
1966. Exotic hardwoods. 28″
high. This sculpture also builds
out architecturally in forms that
are animal, human, and organic,
but it is smooth and precisely
finished.
Courtesy, Dilexi Gallery,
San Francisco

FREYA. George Sugarman. 1964. Laminated, polychromed wood. 30¾" high.
Though most of Sugarman's forms are laminated wood, he is not so concerned
with the material as with the final form. He builds up layers of white pine
that have been cut on a band saw. The form dictates whether screws or dowels
will be used. When people began admiring the grains of the woods, he began
to paint the pieces as an aid to holding the form in space. He uses color, not
as decoration, but to make the piece "work" in space. Color may pull a
piece along, stop it, push it forward, or expand it.

Courtesy, Fischbach Gallery, New York

ORGANIC STUDY. Fred Borcherdt. 1966. Carved walnut. 30″ high. Because the original log had a "crotch," or forked, area, the sculptor had to allow this natural shape to suggest final form.

Photo, author

chapter 5

Direct Carving

Despite contemporary innovations in the artistic use of wood that have structural and architectural aspects, many sculptors still derive their greatest pleasure in carving from a log. The differences between traditional, primitive, and contemporary wood carving may be considered differences in purpose. Wood carving of the past was usually applied decoration; the intricacy of Gothic carvings, for instance, was admired for craftsmanship and technique. Primitive carvers created idols, headgear, and totems for functional purposes and not for art's sake. The contemporary sculptor is interested in an expressive form that combines abstract and representational elements to portray powerful emotions.

The carver invariably feels an emotional involvement with the wood itself. He respects the shape of the log, and works in the long, narrow format imposed by the nature of the material. He is usually eloquent about the natural beauty, texture, graining, tactile quality, warmth, and aroma of wood. There appears to be an indefinable, mystical, sensual force in the carver's relationship to his material.

The beginning carver should progress slowly until he learns the feel of wood and how his tools respond to it. Begin with wood, such as pine, basswood, mahogany, or elm, that is easy to cut and finish. If you cannot find a log, you can buy a piece of 4″ × 4″, 6″ × 6″, or some larger piece of lumber. A well-seasoned, smooth-textured, and evenly colored wood is easiest for the beginner. Knots and other irregularities may be integrated into the form, or ignored.

The majority of experienced carvers emphasize the importance of visualizing the complete form *before* beginning to carve. Make sketches or a clay model of your idea; then adhere to the plan without making major changes.

Chaim Gross cautions students to plan very carefully once they have a piece of wood and form in mind. He tells of the student who wanted to carve a large statue from hardwood but couldn't or wouldn't make a drawing. The student began to carve the 5′ log; and each week the log appeared to shrink, until finally there were only a few inches of wood left, and the student had no statue at all.

A more recent practice is to begin carving without a formal plan, and let the wood itself lead you. Proponents of this philosophy point out that the things that can be done with wood are really very flexible. If you cut away too much, you can glue another form to it, or even have a branch jut out from the form. If the result appears patched or added on, it doesn't matter because the ideal is not necessarily something that must be beautiful and perfect.

Beginning carvers often are afraid to go into wood for fear they'll cut away too much. If they begin with a cube, they believe that

An assortment of carver's tools (beginning from the left): round and half-round rasps, rifflers, chisels, and gouges with blades of different widths and shapes. The handles vary in shape and color, and are weighted according to the size of the tool. A lignum vitae mallet, oil, sharpening stones, sandpaper, and steel wool are all used by the carver.

rounding off the corners makes it a sculpture. It is essential to subtract wood until a new form emerges from the original shape. Adhering to a sketch or model helps to eliminate this problem.

Carvers differ in their treatment of surface textures. Some believe the wood should be smooth and free of toolmarks; others maintain that only toolmarks are compatible with the surface. One sculptor may advocate using any tool, from a penknife to a heavy rasp, to achieve the shape and surface desired; another uses only gouges and chisels, and believes that even sanding violates the wood. Whether the sculptor is nonpurist or purist is really unimportant as far as technique is concerned. The important consideration is the success of the end result.

Such diversified, opposing opinions about wood emphasize the absence of absolute procedures. A sculpture must reflect the essence of the creator's feeling and visions. And these can be infinite. Sculptures that "work" seem to have some mystical, spiritual quality about them that the viewer feels as he responds to the forms and the textures. Of all sculptural form, carving from a log demands exacting advance planning, order, and discipline.

Wood carvings are created in the round, as sculpture, or in high and low relief. This chapter is concerned with sculpture in the

David Hostetler (right) observes a student's progress. The tool shaft is held with one hand and the handle directed with the other for fine work. A mallet (below) is used for heavier work. Assorted logs, hand tools, and a power tool are standard in the carving room. A woodworker's clamp is in the right foreground.

Photo, Ohio University, Athens, Ohio

round that can be viewed from all sides and is unattached to a backing.

TOOLS

The range of tools one can use for carving is wide. The basic cutting tools are knives, chisels, gouges, and rasps, with variations of size and shape. A mallet of hardwood, usually lignum vitae, is used to drive the tool into the wood. Depending upon the size of the sculpture, a holding device may be required. C-clamps, wood clamps, and vises are used to anchor a piece of wood to a workbench. Primitive carvers often hold the wood with their feet, but for obvious reasons this is not recommended. Special work positioners may be screwed to the base of the wood and attached to the workbench. These positioners are on swivels that enable you to turn the wood and work from all sides conveniently. Oddly shaped logs that defy clamping without marking up the wood surface may be anchored by placing the log on two sawhorses, tying it to a tree or post, or propping it with heavy sandbags.

Woodworking gouges and chisels vary in the shape and width of the cutting edge. They include straight, V-shaped to deep spoon shape and tapered, fine-pointed blades. They are classed in three ways: (*a*) shape—straight, curved, or bent; (*b*) width at the cutting edge in inches or millimeters; and (*c*) section—the shape at the cutting edge. A code number is usually stamped on the shaft. Catalogs of woodworking tools list approximately 400 available types of blades.

It is advisable to purchase the best tools you can afford. A good tool, made of high-quality tempered steel, holds a sharp edge and can be resharpened many times. Handles can be replaced if they break under the blow of the mallet. Because some sculptors prefer to make shaped and weighted handles to their own specifications, it is possible to purchase blades separately.

Work with as many tools as you can, and buy those you can control best. However, it is unwise to limit your tool horizon. A sculptor may become so accustomed to a few tools that he never tries others, though he might achieve very desirable and different effects. Handsaws, axes, coping saws, planes, and assorted carpenter's tools should also be part of the sculptor's inventory. The carver should feel free to use any tool that enables him to accomplish what he wants.

Rasps, files, and scrapers are used for blending large areas of form and smoothing surfaces, particularly in hardwood surfaces that will be sandpapered and polished. Files tend to leave deep marks in softwoods. Rasps and files are made in flat, round, half-round, and other shapes. A Surform tool is excellent for removing wood because it cuts clean and does not tear the wood.

Rifflers are small files and rasps curved and tapered at each end. They are used for working into awkward corners and rounded areas.

Some carving is accomplished with power tools. The chain saw, shown in Chapter 2, is great for peeling away bark and sapwood quickly and for roughing out form. Mechanical sanding machines can simplify finishing. Concave shapes within a piece of wood may be beveled by placing a block on the face plate of a lathe and cutting into the wood as it turns. A hand drill, power drill, or drill press can also be used for penetrating wood.

HOW TO SHARPEN TOOLS

Sharp tools are essential for woodcutting. Tools dull and nick quickly if they are not properly handled and cared for. The carver often finds it necessary to sharpen tools that become blunt, nicked, or otherwise defective. (In some areas tools can be brought to professional sharpeners, but this takes time.) A woodcutting chisel is beveled on one edge only, but both edges must be sharp. For hand-sharpening, oilstones are made in various sizes and shapes that fit differently shaped tools. A flat oilstone with a coarse and fine grit is invaluable. Oil is used to lubricate the stone, and the blade is then passed along the stone according to the angle of the blade and the defect to be remedied.

A mechanical grinding stone will sharpen a blade in about an eighth of the time required with oilstones. Generally the sharpening procedure is as follows:

1. Rough-sharpen or grind the tool until the defect or blunt edge is gone and a heavy burr appears. When using a grinding wheel, be particularly careful not to "burn" the edge by letting it become hot, thus causing the tool to lose temper. Constantly dip the tool in oil or cold water to cool it.

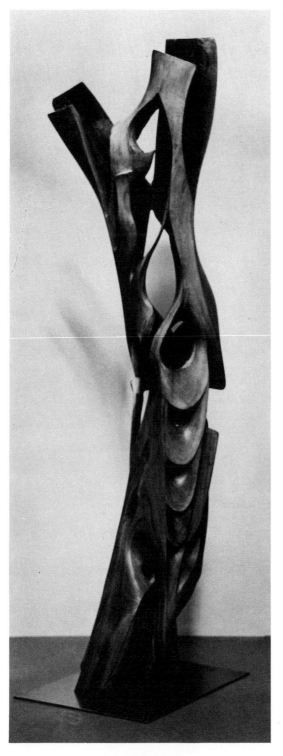

TRAVAIL. Milton Horn. 1962. Walnut. 50″ high. A sculpture in high and low relief is designed to be seen from the front and sides, and is connected to a backing.

Courtesy, artist. Photo, Estelle Horn

ICARUS. Sidney Simon. 1963. Pearwood, 60″ high. Sculpture in the round can be seen from all sides, and must be designed for this consideration.

Courtesy, artist

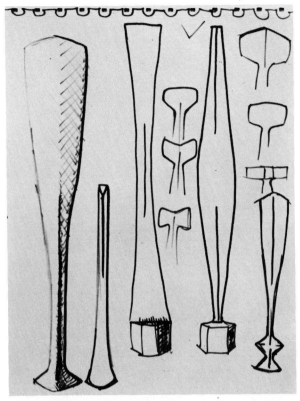

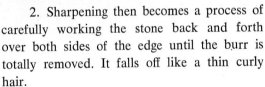

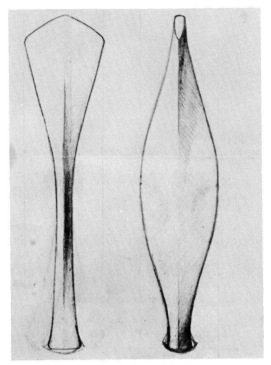

TOTEM II. Fred Borcherdt. Walnut. 5′ high. Sketches at left show the visual development.

Photo, author

2. Sharpening then becomes a process of carefully working the stone back and forth over both sides of the edge until the burr is totally removed. It falls off like a thin curly hair.

3. There are many ways to hold and work the stone and tool when removing the burr. Practice and experience are required before you find the technique that suits you best.

Test the sharpness of a blade by cutting across the grain of a piece of pinewood. A tool may seem to be cutting clean in hardwood, but when tested on soft pine, defects in the cutting edge may be detected more quickly. When testing blades, do not hold the wood in one hand and the tool in the other. A very sharp tool may easily slip off the wood and cut your hand. Never try to catch a falling tool. Whenever you are sharpening and carving, always keep both hands behind the cutting edge to avoid accidents. Wear safety glasses or industrial goggles that cover the sides and front part of your eyes.

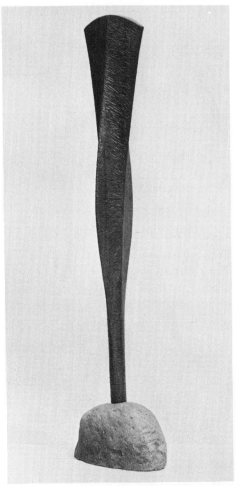

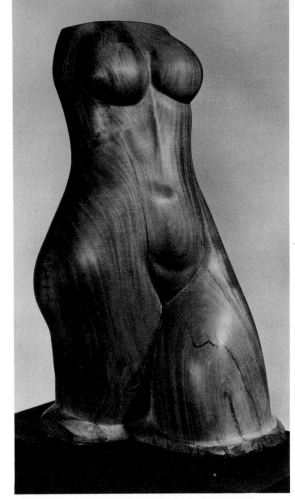

TORSO. Egon Weiner. 1949. Honduras mahogany. Front view and rear view, with preliminary sketches at left. A successful wood sculpture usually takes advantage of simple, broad planes.

Courtesy, artist

THREE-DIMENSIONAL
CONSIDERATIONS OF SCULPTURE

Sculpture is an art of volume, mass, contour, and surface treatment. A sculpture must have volumes organized in space, and the amount of space the sculpture occupies is limited by the original mass of the material. A sculptor confronted with a log or block of timber may retain the greater proportion of the original mass, and the resulting form will be solid and weighty; or he may take away much of the material and thereby lighten the mass, even making negative spaces or holes that allow space to penetrate. When negative space is created, it becomes another element to be considered within the volume of the form.

The character of wood and the tools used make wood carving demanding, hard work.

When an artist develops a visual image for a piece of wood, he must think of it in terms of being seen from all around, from the top and from the bottom. This concept is very different from a two-dimensional painting, for example, that is viewed from the front; and from the relief sculpture that is attached to a background and viewed from the front and sides.

When the artist draws an outline on one side of a piece of wood as a beginning, the outline soon disappears as he begins to carve. If he is working on an oddly shaped log, he is restricted as to design. If he begins to work and finds knots within the log, he may have to alter his form. But no matter what happens, he must consistently subtract material to release the form so it occupies space in a coherent composition. He must constantly refine the design and surface until he successfully transposes the form in his mind's eye to the wood.

THE FAMILY (in progress). Albert Vrana.

THE FAMILY (two views). Albert Vrana. Casuarina wood. 5′ 6″ high. About this piece the artist says: "Most of my wood carving is inspired by inherent true forms and what I imagine in the branching habit of limbs or roots. This piece waited on the carving stand in my studio for almost a year before I decided the best way to use the interesting branching of the tree. The in-process shots (left) show the chip method of carving which I use. I work all over the wood and do not develop any area ahead of another. I think of carving like peeling. This particular wood is very difficult to carve."

Courtesy, artist

WOODEN STATUETTE. Prehistoric. Spiro Mound, Oklahoma. An ancient carving that is representational and symbolic.

Courtesy, Smithsonian Institution, Washington, D.C.

WOODEN ANCESTOR FIGURINE. Easter Islands. Such forms are extremely individualistic. When primitive sculptures first came to the Western artist's attention, the deviations from representational form were a revelation and an inspiration.

Courtesy, Smithsonian Institution, Washington, D.C.

THE HUMAN FIGURE

Until recently, wood sculptures were mainly representational, and limited to human or animal figures. Within this limitation the sculptor was able to create complex arrangements with an astonishing variety of appeal. Whether the artist chose to use wood in a massive, monumental form, or in a light, gay figure, the work contained essential sculptural qualities, such as definite emotional attributes, sensuality, and expression of the artist's involvement. Often the sculpture had religious and other symbolic references.

The human form is still a favorite, though often it may not be particularly representational. As artists were subjected to the influence of science, technology, and mechanization, their sculptures moved through various artistic climates. The human figure gradually assumed the characteristics of the environment. The sweetness of early sculptures was replaced by man struggling against society, against himself, against his environment.

Even if social context was ignored, the human form itself underwent change. Figures became more stylized, more simplified, and were often reduced to such abstract planes that the identity of a figure became obliterated and of less importance.

Important, however, were the new statements the artist was making, and his revision of mass, volume, and planes in relation to space. Henry Moore's "Mother and Child" (page 17) is an early example of the abstraction of human form.

The human figure, ideal for direct carving from a log because it follows the same cylindrical shape, is also a favorite for the constructionist. Examples throughout this book should be studied for the presentation of the human figure within the various disciplines of sculpture.

Each of these sculptures is 30″ high, yet Baskin's work represents a massive monumental solid, textured appearance. Nadelman's "Woman" is light, graceful and smooth. Ideas, form and use of wood are determined by the individuality of the artist and the styles of the times.

SEATED MAN WITH OWL. Leonard Baskin. 1959. Cherry-wood. 30″ high, 16¹⁵⁄₁₆″ wide, 17¾″ deep.
Courtesy, Smith College Museum of Art, Northampton, Massachusetts

DANCING WOMAN. Elie Nadelman. 1918. Probably cherry-wood but heavily stained. Face and neck painted. 30″ high with base.
Courtesy, Wadsworth Atheneum, Hartford, Connecticut.
Photo, E. Irving Blomstrann

MILLY. Sidney Simon. 1959. Black walnut. 34″ high.

Collection, Mrs. Willard Cummings, New York

RITUAL FIGURE. Elbert Weinberg. 1953. Beechwood. 60¼″ high. Some assembling with pegs.

Courtesy, Museum of Modern Art, New York, A. Conger Goodyear Fund.

WOMAN. Elizabeth Catlett. 1959. Cedar.

Courtesy, Museo de Arte Moderne, Mexico

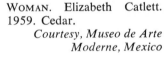

WOMAN. Edward S. Larson. 1967. White pine with water-base stain and matte varnish finish. 8″ high.

Courtesy, artist

Each of these examples utilizes the natural grain and color of the wood. They are all basically solid volume with broad, simple planes. Each figure attests to the obvious craftsmanship of the individual artist and his concern with the potentials and inherent qualities of the wood.

FLUTE PLAYER. Bunni Sovetski. 1948. Honduras mahogany. 50" high.
Collection, Dr. E. Angres, Wilmette, Illinois

WARRIOR. Leonard Baskin. 1964. Walnut.
Collection, Mr. and Mrs. Albert List.
Courtesy, United States Plywood
Corporation, New York

THE APPLE PICKER. Bunni Sovetski. 1948. African mahogany. 50"
high.
        Collection, Mrs. M. Weedon,
                    Chicago.
            Photo, Thornburg

MAN WITH LARGE TEETH. Emil
Gauguin. 1964. Walnut. 48½"
high.
    Courtesy, Kovler Gallery, Chicago.
                Photo, Nickerson

MY DAUGHTER JANE. David
Hostetler. 1965. Elm. 49″ high.
Photo, Jon Webb

RED DRESS. David Hostetler.
1966. Maple. 62″ high.
Photo, Jon Webb

GOD OF THE WIND. Claude Primeau.
1967. Redwood. 6′ high.
Courtesy, Le Québec Art Gallery,
San Francisco

WHO AM I? Sidney Simon. 1966.
Black walnut. 34″ high, 36″ wide.
Courtesy, artist

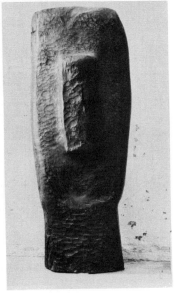

CHI. Kiyoshi Takahashi. 1962.
Madeira wood.
Courtesy, Museo de Arte
Moderne, Mexico

CAPTIVE ANGEL. Elbert Weinberg.
1958. Walnut. 78″ high.
Courtesy, Wadsworth Atheneum,
Hartford, Connecticut.
Photo, E. Irving Blomstrann

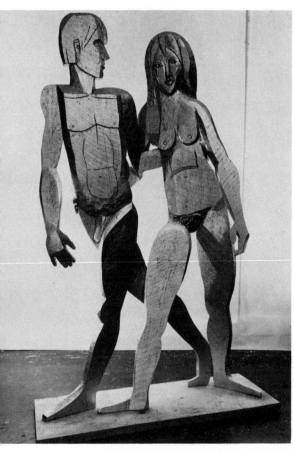

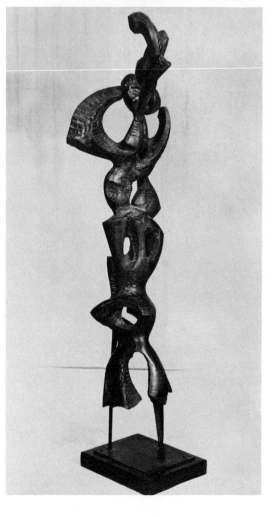

WALKING COUPLE. Anne Arnold.
1966. Carved white pine assembled
and painted with aluminum leaf.
8½′ high.
Courtesy, Fischbach Gallery,
New York.
Photo, Rudolph Burckhardt

ROYAL COUPLE. Roger Majorowicz.
1961. Olive wood. 6′ high.
Courtesy, Feingarten Galleries,
Los Angeles

PAIR OF ANTELOPE HEADPIECES. Africa, Mali Federation, Bambara Tribe. The basic wood-carved figures have been embellished with string, shells, and iron. Male figure 38¾" high, female figure 31¼" high.
Courtesy, Art Institute of Chicago

WOOD CARVING. Igorot Tribe. Philippine Islands.
Courtesy, Smithsonian Institution, Washington, D.C.

THE ANIMAL FORM

Animals have been favorite subjects for the sculptor and painter for centuries. To primitive cultures animals are sacred religious symbols, and a particular animal is often represented in many sculptural ways. It may be as an idol, a headdress, or as a decorative element on a bowl to be used in religious ceremonies. The Thai people, today, consider the elephant a sacred animal, and hundreds of sculptural representations are produced commercially. The cow is sacred to the people of India.

The contemporary sculptor treats animal form in much the same way as human form, moving from representational statements to abstract concepts. By simplifying the shapes of an animal's body, the artist is able to articulate broad planes. Animal images created by primitive cultures often seem as contemporary as those produced by present-day sculptors; or perhaps contemporary sculptors have been so influenced by primitive carvings that they have become eclectic.

Leonard Baskin's human figures often include a bird, owl, or some animal as a mystical, almost surrealistic, symbol. Robert Lockhart combines characteristic parts of different animals in a new animal image, using carving, laminating, and polychrome to present his concept.

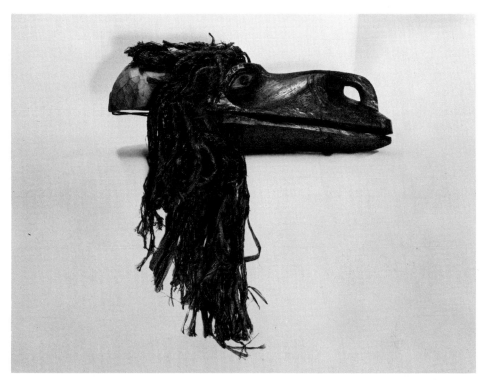

WOODEN MASK. Bella Coola Indians. British Columbia, Canada.
Courtesy, Smithsonian Institution, Washington, D.C.

HIPPO HEAD. Robert Lockhart. 1964.
Courtesy, Kovler Gallery, Chicago. Photo, Nickerson

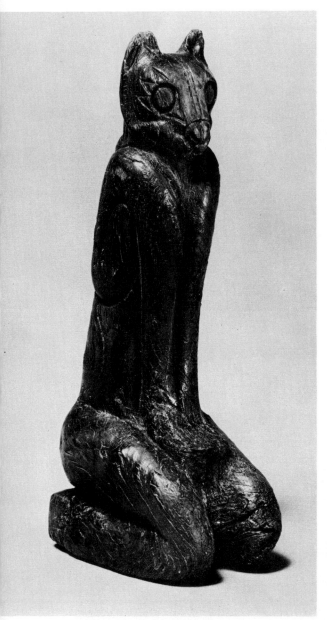

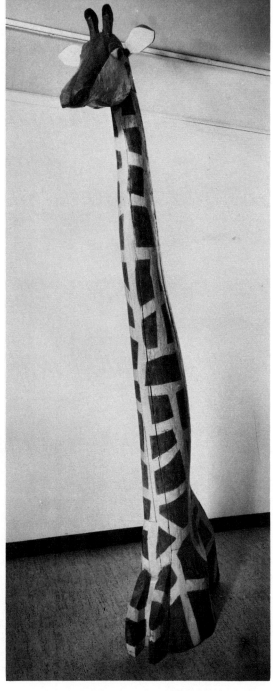

Prehistoric figure of mountain lion or panther man-god. Key Marco, Florida.
Courtesy, Smithsonian Institution, Washington, D.C.

GIRAFFE. Anne Arnold. 1964. Pine, painted. 107″ high. Boards are laminated and carved.
Collection, Mr. and Mrs. Rodrigo Moynihan, Lambesc, Aix, France.
Courtesy, Fischbach Gallery, New York.
Photo, O. E. Nelson

HORNY ANIMAL. Robert Lockhart. 1965. Wood laminated, carved, and polychromed. 5′ high with base.

Courtesy, Kovler Gallery, Chicago.
Photo, Nickerson

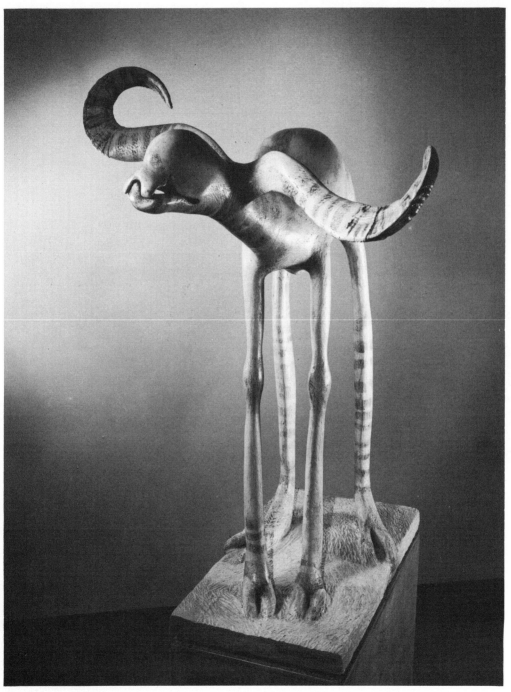

HIPPO COUPLE. Anne Arnold. 1965. Redwood.
Approx. 3½' high, 6½' wide, 6" deep. Sculpture is
built up in three layers and laminated to a backing
board. The carved boards are put together like
pieces of a puzzle.
Courtesy, Sculptors Guild, Inc., New York.
Photo, Rudolph Burckhardt

LARGE BEAR RUG. Robert Lockhart. 48" × 40".
Laminated and built out as in HIPPO COUPLE,
carved and polychromed.
Courtesy, Kovler Gallery, Chicago.
Photo, Nickerson

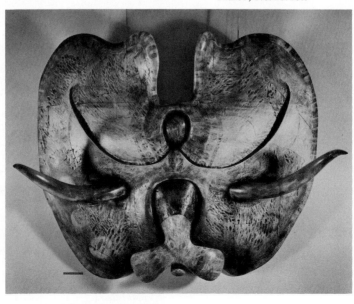

CAT ON A PILLOW. Mark Ulrich. 1966. Black walnut. 5′ long, 3′ high. The artist says: "The theme of the sculpture is unimportant; this idea grew out of a concept of a woman lying on her stomach. What is important is that the shapes function in relation to one another and to space."

Courtesy, artist

SNAIL. Mark Ulrich. 1963–1967. Black walnut. 80″ high.

Courtesy, artist

TOTEM III. Fred Borcherdt. 1967. Walnut. Primitive forms are a definite influence.
Photo, author

CONVOLUTION. Mychajlo R. Urban. 1966. Locust wood with some staining.
Courtesy, artist.
Photo, W. Kacurovsky

NONREPRESENTATIONAL STATEMENTS

As abstract form permeated artistic output, the sculptor, like the painter, began to revise his traditional concepts in subject and methods. It was no longer necessary to retain frankly human or animal representation in the traditional discipline of sculpture. The artist was free to utilize the wood in any way he desired even if it meant penetrating the block for form or burning it for texture. The entire "purist" approach was repudiated.

Many of the following examples have a basis in tradition, but the artist has pushed the potential of wood carving to new statements. He is portraying an emotional feeling that comes from deep within him rather than a recognizable image. Each artist has selected wood as the medium because of its quality of projecting a warmth and an inherent kind of life to a concept that might otherwise be cold and impersonal if created from metal or carved from stone. Each artist has an obvious respect for the material. He is highly competent in dealing with the nature of wood and in manipulating shapes and surface treatments.

HOUSE OF BIRTH. Fred Powell.

Courtesy, Feingarten Galleries, Los Angeles

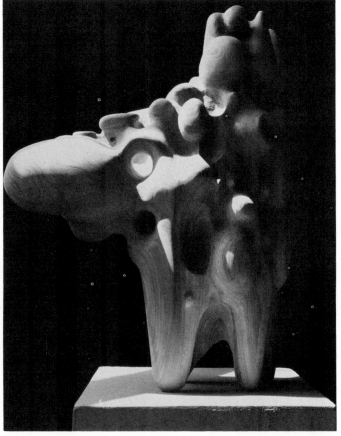

UNTITLED. Gary Wojcik. 1967.
Walnut. 2' high.
Courtesy, artist

SHAPES OF A DREAM. Mychajlo
R. Urban. 1966. Elmwood.
Courtesy, artist

AWESOME GROWTH. Dennis Kowal, Jr. 1967. Walnut. 30″ high.

Courtesy, artist

HOMAGE TO ARP. Dennis Kowal, Jr. 1966. Walnut. 28″ high.
Courtesy, artist

118

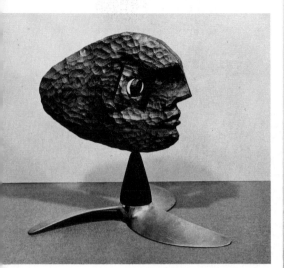

THE CRITIC. Sidney Simon. 1965. Black walnut with metal propeller. 18″ × 18″ without propeller. The head shape is carved from 2″ board, but varying gouge marks and treatment give feeling of deep round form. The eyepiece moves within the head.

Courtesy, artist

TRIO. Masha Solomon. Padouk and mahogany. 14″ high. Carved forms assembled.
Courtesy, Ruth White Gallery,
New York.
Photo, Eric Pollitzer

COLOR PLATES OPPOSITE:

EYE. John Little. 1967.
Painted pine. 64″ high.
Photo, John Reed

COCKTAIL TABLE. Robert C. Whitley.
Walnut. 42″ diameter.
Courtesy, artist

THE CANTERBURY TALES. Stanley Kaplan.
Philippine mahogany carved.
The Levittown Memorial High School Library, New York.
Courtesy, artist

PAINTED WOOD SCULPTURES ON EXHIBIT.
Forman Onderdonk. 1966—67.
Courtesy, artist

ASSEMBLAGE. Robert Pierron. 1967.
Pine, charred and painted. 24″ × 30″.
Collection, Dr. and Mrs. Melvin Meilach, Chicago.
Photo, author

THIRTEEN CATS. Bernard Langlais.
1967. 48″ × 96″. *Courtesy, artist*

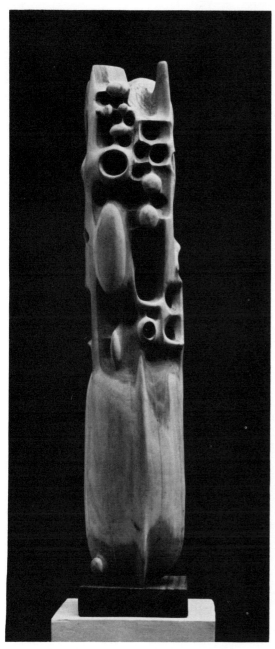

TOWER. Mychajlo R. Urban. 1967. Locust wood.

Courtesy, artist

RENAISSANCE HOUSE. Claude Primeau. 1967. Redwood. 6' high.

Courtesy, artist

WOOD MOSAIC. L. Stanley Carpenter. Wood blocks and scrap pieces are arranged to utilize the textures of cut surfaces and end grains. Drilled holes serve as a negative repeat of the circular forms in the rough-sawed dowels. For additional texture, some sawdust is also glued to the assemblage.

Courtesy, artist.
Photo, Richard Gross

chapter 6.

Assemblage of Found and Weathered Wood

Nature, once having produced wood, does not relent in her effect upon it after it has fallen from the tree. Wood scraps, weathered by sand, water, sun, and myriad other elements, assume appearances that man cannot duplicate. In a single piece of driftwood there are unimaginable ridges, shapes, colors, and textures. Scrap pieces of weathered wood are assembled by many sculptors into highly original, expressive works of art.

Wooden parts rescued from old buildings, discarded furniture, and other objects that have supposedly outlived their usefulness are being used increasingly. The challenge of giving a new existence or new context to cast-off items is a continuing one for many artists who rebel at the built-in obsolescence of our society.

Often a wooden part from an old object will evoke emotions. A piece of ornate carving from a cornice, the trim from a dresser, a bedpost or banister newels lovingly turned by some anonymous craftsman may represent nostalgia. By utilizing these fractured, fragmented, skeletal forms and combining them into new relationships the artist arrives at a new meaning and, at the same time, expresses personal emotions.

The artist may use wood scraps as he finds them, or he may cut, carve, and paint them. He may combine them with other materials such as iron, paper, shells, plastic, or glass, or use any other assortment of objects for his composition. Much of the scrap weathered wood is found by beachcombing, by scavenging about old building sites or in secondhand

121

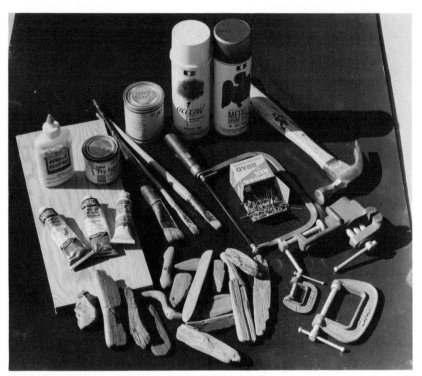

Much material for wood assemblage may be found in every
home workshop. A plank of plywood, Masonite, or canvas board
may be used for the backing of a relief assemblage. Glues, paints,
hammers, nails, saw, and clamps are useful, as are the various
pieces of wood with their different shapes, textures, and grains.

Photo, author

furniture stores. Yet each bit of material is
carefully selected for texture and color.

There is nothing haphazard about the
use of assorted materials. They are combined
in relationships that must conform to the elements of composition. Such assemblage is not
considered a "purist" art form because of the
scope of materials and experiences. Yet the
assembler frequently develops his own guide-
lines for creating an artistically coherent piece
of work.

When you find wood scraps, look beyond
what the piece was or is. Search for new images in the forms and how they relate to
another object or shape. To the trained artistic
mind and eye a piece of wood with a dark

knot, pronounced grain, and weathered holes
can have meaning and beauty; to the un-
trained it may be just another piece of junk to
be kicked aside. A root or branch may be so
shaped that it will in itself suggest the form of
a bird or animal. It has volume, and exists in
space, so that, by recognition, it becomes sculptural form.

Assemblage is an easy way to begin
working with wood. Technical knowledge of
the material is not required. Pieces may be cut
with a coping saw or band saw. Some additional treatment may be given by using the
techniques that are discussed in the following
pages. Then it's simply a matter of arranging
the pieces in an artistic manner.

SHELL GAME. Robert Pierron.
1967.

Photo, author

OBJET EN BOIS. Jaap Wage-
maker. 1961. Wood with metal
parts.

*Courtesy, Galerie Delta
Rotterdam, Holland*

Bernard Langlais often creates large assemblages by using old planks for backing and cutouts of assorted old and new wood with different colors and textures. He builds up several layers of wood in some portions and leaves other areas of one or two layers. He may cut through some of the backing.

Where necessary he carves with a mallet and chisel.

Or an ax. The final assemblage has natural wood and painted portions.

Photo series, courtesy, artist

Cows (THE GIRLS). Bernard
Langlais. 48″ × 52″.
Courtesy, artist. Photo, Peter Moore

In another theme of farm animals,
Langlais sketches a shape for a
multilayered area.

SKY CATHEDRAL. Louise Nevelson. 1948. Wood construction painted black.
11'3½" high, 10'¼" wide, 1'6" deep.

Courtesy, Museum of Modern Art, New York.
Gift of Mr. and Mrs. Ben Mildwoff

MATE. Robert Indiana. 1960–1962. Wood and mixed media. 41″ high, 12½″ wide, 12¾″ deep.
Courtesy, Whitney Museum of American Art, New York

NATURAL SELECTIVITY. Dona Meilach. 1968. 9″ × 12″. Wood found along beach, and dried. Assembled with pink stone on green canvas board. Hand-carved wood frame, Mexico.

Photo, author

Artist Robert Pierron has developed several techniques for controlling texture and color and for simulating weathered wood (for the finished composition on page 130, SLIVERS). Pierron begins by making a paper design, and then transposes the pattern to a piece of 5-ply plywood. He numbers the positions on the wrong side of the wood according to the pattern. The pieces are cut on a band saw.

With a screwdriver and a hammer he shreds each piece by prying away one or two layers of the plywood. Because plywood laminations are in alternating directions, the grain of each layer is different. (If you place the numbers of the design on the top side of the wood, they will disappear in the shredding process.)

Next, he burns the shredded surface lightly with a torch. This brings up the grain beautifully. It also softens the ragged edges and blends the laminations to resemble a natural weathering process such as water erosion might create.

He uses a stiff brush to clear the burned ash from the wood.

Some pieces are rubbed with manganese blue oil paint, which gives the wood a bluish-green tint. Others remain in the natural burned tones.

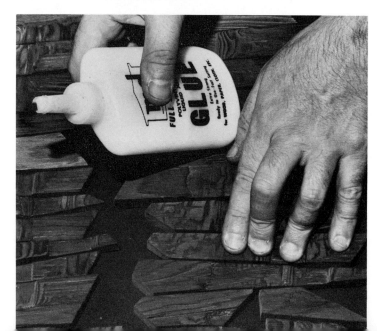

The pieces are then glued onto a backboard in the arrangement originally determined by the sketch. (The numbers are still on the backs for identification.) Notice the various layers and grains achieved.

SLIVERS. Robert Pierron. 1967. Plywood cut, burned, and reassembled.
Photo, author

BLACK ISLAND. Robert Pierron. 1967. Shredded burned plywood.
Photo, author

TOOTH AND NAIL. Bernard Langlais. 1962. Wood
painting. 4′ × 4′.
Courtesy, Allan Stone Galleries, Inc., New York.
Photo, Rudolph Burckhardt

IN BETWEEN. Michael Rothenstein.
Courtesy, Tate Gallery, London

A Royal Portrait #2. Jacqueline Fogel. 1964. Wood parts from posts, furniture, moldings, and so on, cut, carved, and polychromed. 15″ × 20¼″.

Collection, Mr. and Mrs. Sanford Klapholz, New York.
Photo, Rupert Finegold

FROM THE SEA. Dona Meilach. 1968. Found wood with shells and stones on black painted canvas board. 8″ × 10″.

Photo, author

SAND FOUNTAIN WITH WHITE SAND. Ann Wiseman. 1965. 17″ × 9″.
Collection, Chase Manhattan Bank, New York.
Photo, Jan Jachniewicz

UNTITLED. Michael Drucks. 1967.
Courtesy, Gordon Gallery, Tel Aviv, Israel.
Photo, Micha Hahn

FISH. Jacob Burck. 1966. Wooden basket parts, pegboard, and scrap wood, with car headlight for eye and saw blade for teeth.
Courtesy, Conrad Gallery, Chicago

ONE AND OTHERS. Louise Bourgeois. 1955. Painted and stained wood. 20¼" high.
Courtesy, Whitney Museum of American Art, New York. Photo, O. E. Nelson

TUNNEL OF LOVE. Sidney Simon. 1962. Mobile made from an old rain barrel and assorted carved wood figures.
Collection, Laurence Bloedal, Williamstown, Massachusetts

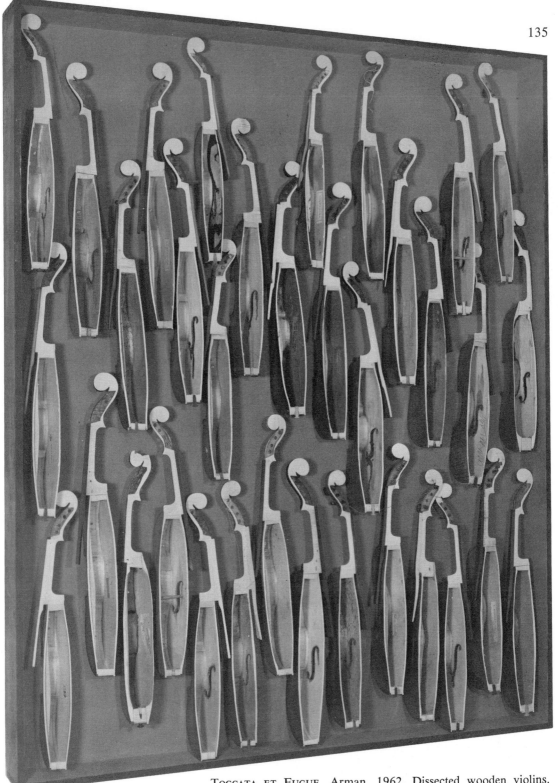

TOCCATA ET FUGUE. Arman. 1962. Dissected wooden violins. 65″ × 52½″.

Courtesy, Albright-Knox Art Gallery, Buffalo, New York. Gift of Seymour H. Knox

UPRISE. John Townsend. Wood wall relief, constructed and carved and painted white. 48¾″ high, 57¾″ wide.

Courtesy, Chase Manhattan Bank, New York.

Photo, Jan Jachniewicz

chapter 7

Wood Constructions in Relief

In the previous chapter, materials determined form and composition. The inherent nature of a shape of wood became the dominating part of the work. In this chapter, examples illustrate designs that are first visualized by the artist, who then constructs the wood to carry out that visualization. Relief, where objects project from a background, may be high or low or a combination of both. The artist must always be concerned with the contrasts of light and shade created by the shapes.

Historically, relief design was carved from a backing, as in the marble friezes of the Parthenon. Carved friezes in wood and stone were most often used on buildings to tell a story or as decorative imagery. Traditionally, such carvings were composed of human and animal forms.

The contemporary artist also carves, but very often he also constructs a relief as an object to be hung on a wall, like a painting, or attached to the wall, like a mural (see Chapter 11). He may laminate, join woods by carpentering, and then carve. His ideas are likely to include organic, geometric, literary, mechanical, and abstracted human and animal connotations.

Line, a basic element of art, is more important and easier to achieve in wood-relief constructions than in any other category of wood sculpture. The nature of wood prevents it from being developed into thin lines such as can be created with metal or by drawing. In carving, line can be suggested but not really developed as line. In relief constructions, however, edges of lumber, moldings, and thin dowels can be cut and placed so that line can be developed for direction and size, to produce various emotions. Lines carry out movement in the positive and negative light and dark areas. They may be continuous or broken, and interplay with varying degrees of harmony and contrast between the shapes and their shadows.

Surface treatment of wood may be as varied as the compositions themselves. Textures are created by cutting, drilling, sanding rough and smooth, scraping, shredding, splintering, and burning. Color may be monotone or vivid. It may be achieved by staining, painting with brush or spray, by burning, or in many combinations. The techniques demonstrated have been developed because artists continually attempt to discover different things they can do with materials.

Because wood can be cut into infinite sizes and shapes, used natural or painted, its potential for relief constructions is still considered at the threshold of artistic exploration.

To create the relief construction at right, Robert Pierron demonstrates his methods for treating wood. Here he uses 2″ × 4″ and 1″ × 2″ pieces of common pine board. A design is traced on the boards, and the pieces are cut on a band saw. Certain angles can also be cut on a band saw; the wood can also be rasped and sanded.

Next, the pieces are burned with a torch to bring out the grain. You can see the difference between the burned and natural surface. (A propane or oxyacetylene torch may be used.)

Then the ash is brushed from the burned area and the grain is accentuated.

Each piece is sprayed with a flat black paint and, when dry, is wire-brushed again to remove some of the color and bring out the patterns of the grain more definitely. The pieces of wood are laid out to show how they were cut from the pine.

UNTITLED. Robert Pierron. 1968. Pine mounted on plywood painted white.

Photo, author

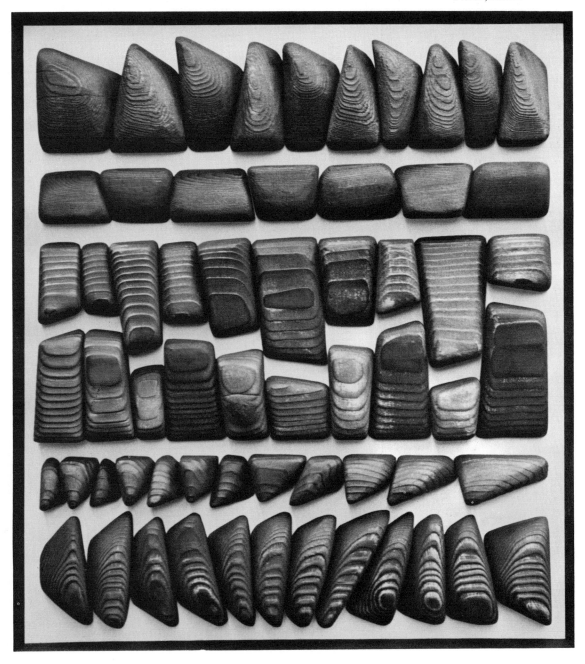

140

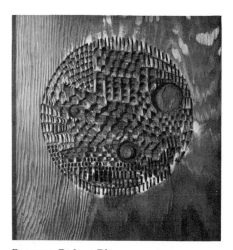

PLANET. Robert Pierron.
1967. Plywood.

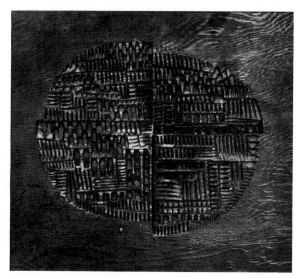

PLANET I. Robert Pierron.
1967. Plywood.

Robert Pierron also uses a technique that he terms "tool burning"; it may be applied to the types of compositions he has developed here or to any other wood surface where a similar texture is desired. It consists of fashioning tool points, which are then heated and impressed into the wood.

CITYSCAPE I. Robert Pierron.
1967. Plywood.

A design is developed on paper, then traced on a piece of plywood.

Some of the tools are screwdrivers that have been reshaped on a grinding wheel to give different effects; some are pointed, some rounded, some angled, and so forth. Other tools are made from small pieces of metal with nails welded to the backs. When these pieces are heated, hold them with a vice-grip pliers. Screwdrivers already have heat-resistant handles.

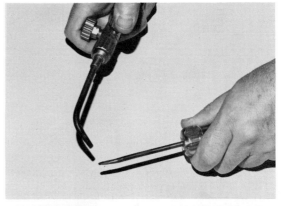

The tool is heated with an oxy-acetylene torch fitted with a small tip. Heat until the metal tool tip is white hot.

Press the heated tool tip into wood immediately. Reheat as necessary to create patterns. Here you can see the indentations made in the plywood. The outer portion of the plywood was also burned to bring out texture. Always brush away the ash with a wire brush. Color may be rubbed in if desirable.

Photos, author

ORIENTAL #2. Robert Pierron. 1967. Shredded and burned pieces of plywood cut and assembled. Color rubbed in with manganese blue oil paint.

Photo, author

WHITE WOOD RELIEF. Sergio Camargo.
Courtesy, Tate Gallery, London

WHITE RELIEF. Ben Nicholson. 1935. Carved from mahogany, mounted on plywood, and painted white. The precise geometrical shapes rely on the subtle shadow contrasts created in the monochromed composition.

Courtesy, Tate Gallery, London

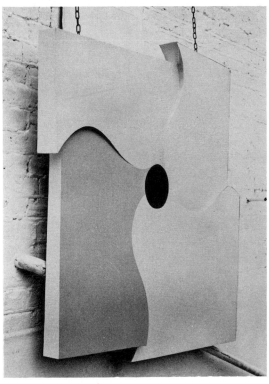

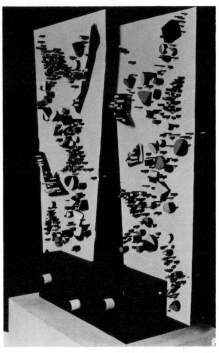

ECLIPSE: VIEW 2. Audrey Skaling. 1966. Carved wooden parts assembled in relief, and painted.
Courtesy, Ruth White Gallery, New York.
Photo, Brenwasser

QUARTET. Alan Green. 1966. Painted wood. 48″ × 50″.
Courtesy, Hamilton Galleries Ltd.,
London

ECLIPSE IMAGE (Box #30). Robert Eshoo. Wooden box with wood parts and glass. 16″ high, 24″ wide, 5¼″ deep.
Courtesy, Chase Manhattan Bank, New York.
Photo, Jan Jachniewicz

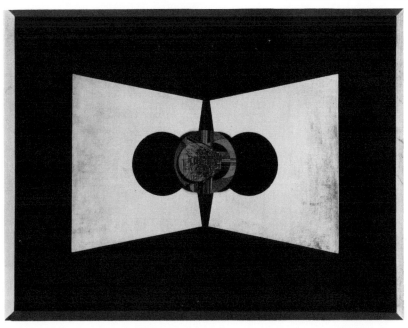

DRIFT. Irwin Gwyther. 1967.
Balsawood on blockboard.
*Courtesy, Gimpel Fils Gallery
Ltd., London*

WOOD MOSAIC #4. Ralph Koester. Painted
black and white. 25″ high, 43½″ wide.
*Courtesy, Chase Manhattan Bank, New York.
Photo, Jan Jachniewicz*

SPHEREMUSIC 2. John Willenbecher. 1966.
Wood construction. 41¼″ high, 43½″ wide.
*Courtesy, Richard Feigen Gallery, New York.
Photo, Geoffrey Clements*

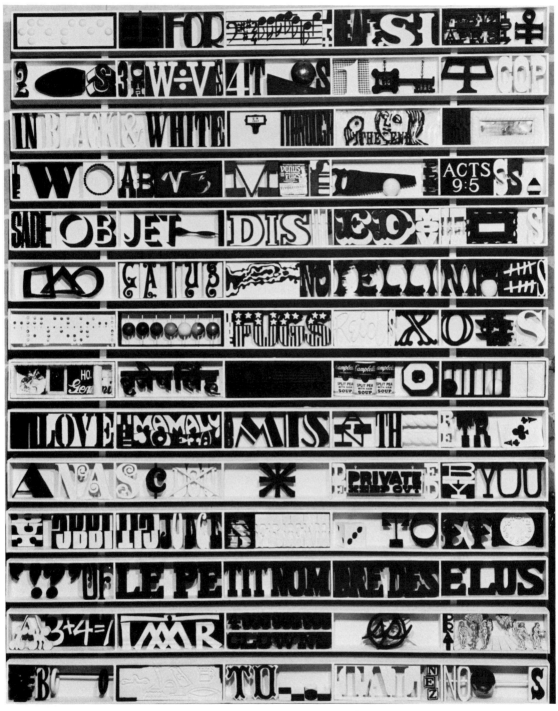

SONNET. James Russell. 1967. Cut wood shapes on Masonite. Painted with acrylic. 78″ high, 60″ wide, 4″ deep. This large construction has literary conception. It is divided into fourteen lines of five poetic feet each, as is a sonnet. The parts within each foot may be read like a rebus puzzle, with connotations from James Joyce.

Collection, Lawrence Majewski, New York

BIG DADDY. Forman Onderdonk. 1967. Pine laminated and joined by various techniques and painted. 5′ high.

Photo, author

chapter 8

Sculptural Constructions — Three-Dimensional

The esthetic aspects of three-dimensional sculpture have been discussed in relation to direct carving (Chapter 5). A three-dimensional sculpture can be seen from all sides, and depends upon masses, broad planes, and their relationship to space. A sculptural construction occupies space much as a building does, and is, in many ways, architectural. As the artist moved away from the limitations of the cylindrical log and into sculpture with architectural monumentality, he extended forms and thrust them in and out of space. His articulations often include hand- and machine-made methods. Frequently the sculptural constructions combine wood with other materials such as steel, plastic, and fabrics. A wood construction may serve as a shell for kinetics, light, and other technological aspects that are part of the contemporary art scene.

Some constructionists rely on natural wood tones and grains; others use wood as does the carpenter whose construction ultimately will be painted. A colorist believes that the spatial dimensions of sculptural planes afford shifting color relationships that are unobtainable on a flat painted surface. David Smith often began by making a painting, then placing the colors on a construction as though he knocked out space. Such constructions were meant to be viewed mainly from the front, yet color was used all around.

Sculpture also is free to be deceptive, and this can be accomplished by manipulating wood planes by means of direction and color, mirrors, light, motion, and so on. Mirrors and color, for instance, can create illusions similar to those an interior decorator applies to alter room proportions visually.

All methods of wood joining discussed earlier are employed in construction. In fact, simplified large sculptures that fall into the "minimal" sculpture category have become almost completely carpentry projects. The artist may conceive the form on paper, draw up specifications, then order the piece built.

Sculptors constantly argue as to whether or not such practice constitutes total artistic involvement. Must the sculptor create the work from inception of idea to finished product? Or is artistic function satisfied as long as the artist conceives the idea and oversees its creation? How many artists, for example, pour their own bronze castings? And if they don't, does this make them any less the artist?

Regardless of one's position in the argument, the following examples present current activity in this growing sculptural development.

UNTITLED. Roger Barnes. Assembled wooden boxes with laminated forms within. Some painting.
Courtesy, Fairweather-Hardin Gallery, Chicago

UNTITLED #1. Roger Barnes. 1966. Wood construction with laminated wood top and base. 8' high.
Courtesy, Fairweather-Hardin Gallery, Chicago

BAMBU. Roland López Dirube. 1962. Bamboo wood. 60" high. Basically, the sculpture utilizes the cylindrical tree trunk, but constructions are cut out and extended away from the base, with other parts added.
Courtesy, artist

TOTEMIC STRUCTURE. Patricia Fulford. 1967. Stark
arrangements of painted wood blocks.
Courtesy, Mazelow Gallery, Toronto,
Ontario, Canada

INTERMINGLING SPHERES. L. Schanker. Oak. 31" high.
Courtesy, Sculptors Guild, Inc., New York.
Photo, Walter Rosenblum

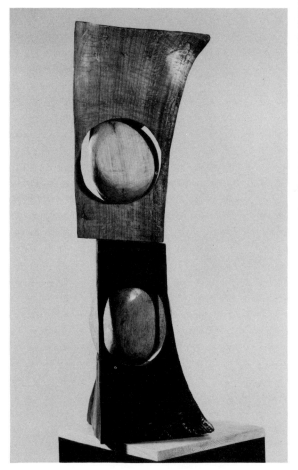

THE FAMILY. Mike Nevelson. Laminated constructions are larger than life. They are smoothly finished, with parts that open and close.

Courtesy, artist

FOR GIACOMETTI. Mark di Suvero. 1962. Personal symbolism is involved in this construction of wood, steel, and iron. 44″ high, 3′ wide, 6′ long.

Courtesy, Wadsworth Atheneum, Hartford, Connecticut.
Photo, E. Irving Blomstrann

DREAM IN PRIMARIES.
Mychajlo Urban.
1967. Locust and applewood. 30″ high.
Courtesy, artist

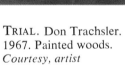

TRIAL. Don Trachsler.
1967. Painted woods.
Courtesy, artist

THE CELLO PLAYER. Jacqueline Fogel.
Found wood assemblage. 28″ high.
Courtesy, The Krasner Gallery, New York.
Photo. Rupert Finegold

UNTITLED.
Richard Kowal. 1967. Mahogany laminated. 30″ high.
Photo, Brian Katz

ICE BUCKET.
Robert G. Trout. Walnut.
Photo, Marshall LaCour

BUST.
Ralph Noel Dagg. 1966. Black Walnut. 16″ high.
Courtesy, artist

LUNAR ARCHITECTURE #2. Eduardo Ramírez. 1966. Painted wood. 31″ × 39″.
Courtesy, Graham Gallery, New York.
Photo, Rudolph Burckhardt

DOXIE. Jeremy Anderson. A combination of animal and airplane shapes results in a humorous commentary on contemporary society.
Courtesy, San Francisco Museum of Art

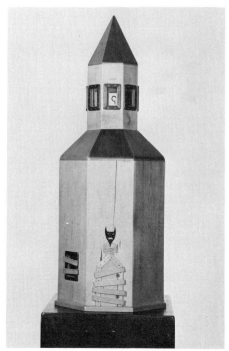

UNTITLED. Arnold Cherullo. 1967. Pine
and mixed woods cut on a band saw and
doweled and glued.

Courtesy, artist

MYSTERIOUSLY ABANDONED IN NEW
HOME. H. C. Westermann. 50″ high.
Courtesy, Art Institute of Chicago.
Gift of Lewis Manilow

BLACK-AND-WHITE SIGNAL #2. Fred Troller. 1965.
Painted wood. 65″ high, 9′ wide, 29″ deep.
Courtesy, Grace Borgenicht Gallery, Inc.,
New York

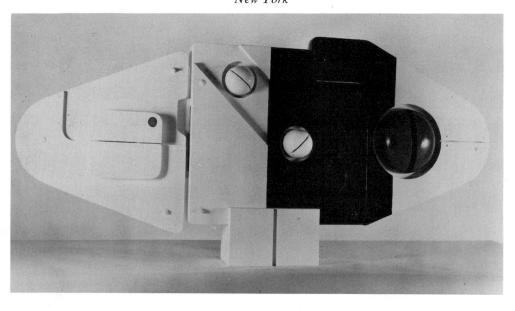

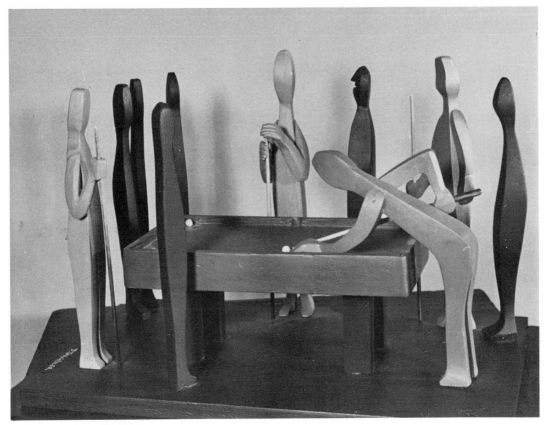

THE BALL PLAYERS. Don Trachsler.
1967. Figures cut on a band saw,
painted.
Courtesy, artist

UNTITLED. Ronald Bladen. 1966.
Wood to be made into metal. 8'
high, 8' wide, 16' long.
Courtesy, Fischbach Gallery,
New York

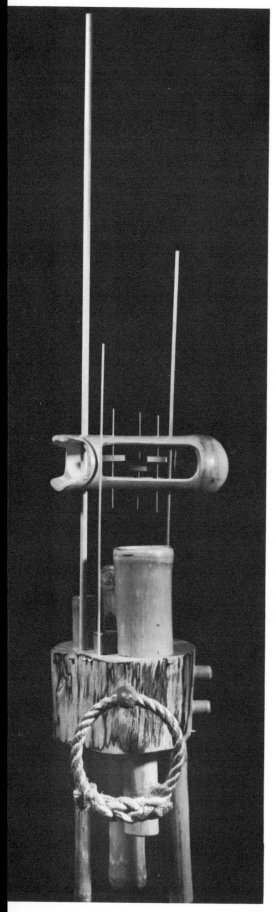

UNTITLED. Rolando López Dirube. 1963. Bamboo, teakwood, and princewood, or *baría* (a Cuban hardwood). 5'2" high.

Courtesy, artist

A SMALL NEGATIVE THAUGHT. H. C. Westermann. 1962. Douglas fir. 28" high. Westermann considers himself an artist of the present, but he values traditional construction methods. He is particularly sensitive to the grain and color of wood. His works are sculpturally potent, and have great psychological implications.

Courtesy, Wadsworth Atheneum, Hartford, Connecticut.
Photo, E. Irving Blomstrann

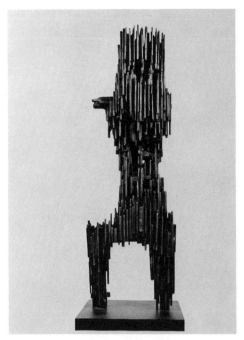

MATHER. David Packard. 1960. Wood blocks laminated. 4′ high.
Collection, Mr. and Mrs. Irving Forman, Chicago

WARRIOR. David Packard. 1960. Wood blocks and objects.
Collection, Mr. Silverberg, New York

UNTITLED. Arnold Cherullo. 1967. Pine Some white acrylic painting. 20″ high.
Courtesy, artist

THE HOOPING HOLLOW. Hans Hokanson. 1965. Natural-color wood with portions painted yellow, white, and green. Basic log forms are constructed. 50″ high.
Courtesy, Fischbach Gallery, New York.
Photo, Val Telberg

156

SWEETHEART 1963. Charles Frazier. 1963.
Wood with lacquer. 16¾″ high.
Courtesy, Whitney Museum of American Art,
New York. Gift of the
Howard and Jean Lipman Foundation, Inc.

SYMPAN. Michael Lekakis. 1960. Oak. 86″ high.
Courtesy, Whitney Museum of American Art,
New York. Gift of the
Friends of the WMAA

EIGHT. John Goodyear. 1966. Wood, enamel, light, glass.
24¼″ high, 48½″ wide, 8″ deep.
Courtesy, Whitney Museum of American Art, New York.
Gift of Joseph L. Shulman

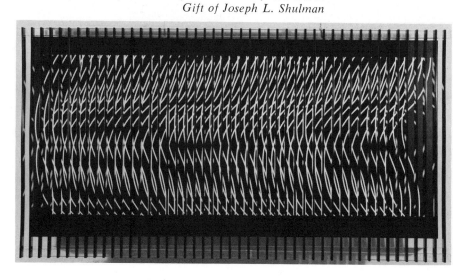

SUNBATHERS. Marisol. 1967. Wood and mixed media. Marisol is known for her keen observations, which find expression through a highly individualistic sense of humor.

Courtesy, Sidney Janis Gallery, New York.
Photo, Geoffrey Clements

4 IN ONE, 5 BY 6½. Melvin Johnson. 1961–1962. Painting on wood construction.

Courtesy, Art Institute of Chicago

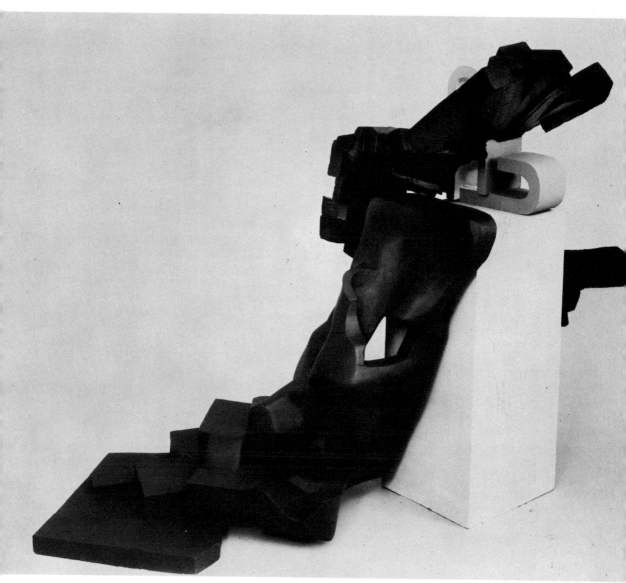

RITUAL PLACE. George Sugarman. 1964–1965. Laminated, polychromed wood sculpture. 5½′ long, 4′2″ high. Sugarman's figures seem to evolve effortlessly—an appearance that belies the work required to create this feeling.

Courtesy, Fischbach Gallery, New York

PART II— FUNCTIONAL OBJECTS

CLOCKS AND TABLE. Pedro Friedeberg. Clocks are made of wood with high color, highly enameled surfaces.

Courtesy, Ontario East Gallery, Chicago

chapter 9.

Accessories

Today, it is impractical to draw a line between craftsman and artist. The separation appears to be one of vacillating and questionable definition: the craftsman makes "utilitarian" objects, while the artist makes nonfunctional objects that are, for lack of a better term, called "fine" arts.

The craftsman employs techniques and designs that are useful in art. The artist, in turn, uses many techniques of the crafts. Furthermore, many artists have turned their talents to useful objects. Picasso has made pottery, Giacometti, lamps; Calder, kitchen utensils and surrealist chess sets; William Accorsi and many others have made toys.

Certainly, the following examples of small, useful wood objects illustrate the close affinity between the two professions. Each object exists in space and has sculptural mass and volume combined with ingenious creativity and respect for material. The simplicity of contemporary design, like sculpture, often draws its inspiration from primitive carvings. Accessories, too, have undergone style changes from baroque to romantic to modern.

Techniques used for creating individual, custom household accessories are the same as those discussed throughout the book. Some of the pieces are carved directly from a log and are completely handmade, using only chisels, gouges, and smoothing papers. Some are constructed by using joints and glues. Many are laminated to combine different kinds of woods, and are then carved by hand or machine. Lathes and mechanical sanders are widely used.

A knowledge of the properties of various woods is essential for creating useful objects. It would be pointless, for instance, to make a cutting board of anything but the hardest woods because of the uses to which it will be put. Finishing techniques are important both to seal the wood and to make it impervious to water, oils, or detergents and soaps. If a bowl is to be made of laminated pieces of wood, a waterproof glue must be used so that the piece will withstand washing.

WOOD BOWLS. Solomon Islands.
Hand-carved with some inlay work.
*Courtesy, Smithsonian Institution,
Washington, D.C.*

BOWL. Robert G. Trout. Vermilion
with birch inlay. Bowl turned on
a lathe.

Photo, Marshall LaCour

BOWL. Robert G. Trout. Vermilion
with birch inlay. Bowl turned and
carved.

Photo, Marshall LaCour

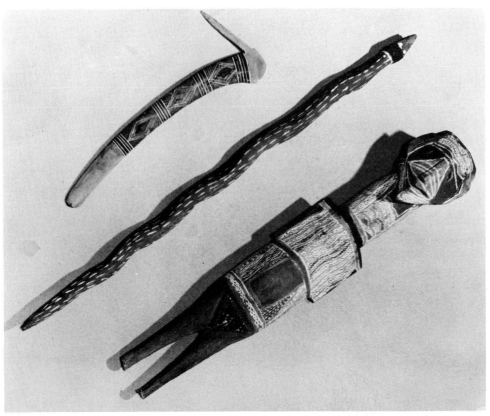

Carved and painted boomerang (top). Carved ceremonial python (center). Wooden ceremonial figure (bottom). Australia.

Courtesy, Smithsonian Institution, Washington, D.C.

WAR CLUB MODEL. Fred Borcherdt. 1967. Walnut with glued ebony and a whale's tooth. The design was created by heating an instrument and impressing it into the wood.

Photo, author

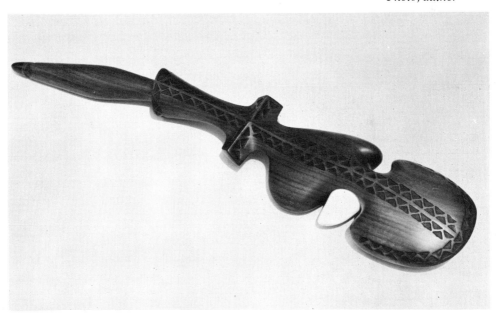

DECORATING TECHNIQUES

After a bowl or other object has been shaped on a lathe, with a saw or by hand-gouging, there are many ways in which it may be decorated. The demonstrations are simply different applications of some of the techniques shown for sculpture.

A design may be carved by using one of the small, motorized hand-held grinding tools. A variety of interchangeable cutters will result in wide, narrow, beveled, pinpoint, or other types of cuts. This handy tool makes carving faster, easier, and more dependable than hand-carving. Harder woods are more easily carved with this tool than they can be carved by hand.

Tool, Courtesy, Dremel,
Racine, Wisconsin

Designs may also be burned with a burning tool that heats electrically. Points of different shapes may also be used. Preshaped tools you create yourself (see Chapter 7) may be heated with a propane or oxyacetelyne torch and pressed into the wood. Shaped wire forms heated and pressed into the wood in a repeat pattern are used by Polish craftsmen for this typical folk art used in many wooden accessories.

Beautiful inlay may be accomplished by using pegs and dowels. (See Chapter 4.) A round peg or peg of some other shape is placed into a hole drilled or shaped by the hand grinder in the same shape as the peg. (Robert Trout uses this technique.) The peg is made of wood different from that of the bowl so the color and grain differ.

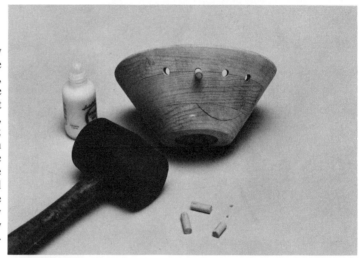

The peg is glued, then lightly tapped into the hole. Forcing the peg may cause the bowl to crack, particularly if it is laminated. (Use a waterproof glue if the object must withstand many washings.) Here, the hole is drilled straight through; the peg will appear round on both the inner and outer surfaces. If the hole were drilled on an angle, the peg would become oval in the final placement. On a thick surface the peg may be placed in a shallow depression so it appears on only one surface, as with traditional inlay work.

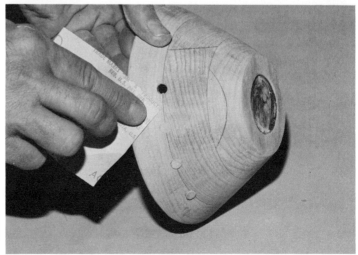

The peg is sanded. After wax, stain, or other finish is applied, the peg becomes the decoration because of the different woods and grains.

BOB STOCKSDALE TURNS A BOWL

1 Sawing out the blank on the tilted table of the band saw.

4 Before the inside of the bowl is turned, a depth hole is drilled to act as a guide.

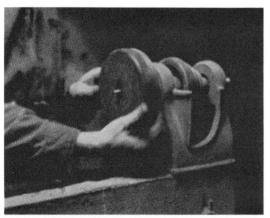

2 Mounting on the lathe the faceplate to which the blank is attached.

5 Faceplate is removed from the lathe and remounted on the bottom of the bowl.

3 Turning begins. First the sides are tapered; here the bottom is turned flat.

Photos, courtesy of Bob Stocksdale, from Craft Horizons, *October 1956 issue*

6 Bowl in place on lathe, the tool rest is adjusted preparatory to roughing out.

7 Rough turning that hollows out the form creates a veritable cascade of wood chips.

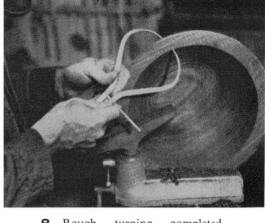

8 Rough turning completed, thickness is checked with calipers before fine turning commences.

9 For safety, Stocksdale wears plastic face guard when turning, respirator when sanding.

10 Finally, faceplace is removed, screw holes are plugged, and bowl then gets overnight oil bath.

Assorted bowls showing various grains and
shapes. Robert Stocksdale.

Courtesy, artist

BOWL. Robert Stocksdale. Turned on a lathe
and hand finished.

Courtesy, artist

WALNUT BOWL. Eben Warren Haskell.
Courtesy, artist

TEAK BOWL. Jerry Glaser.
Courtesy, artist

BOWLS. George Federoff. French walnut with walrus and mastodon ivory inlay (top). African cherry, with walrus handle and mastodon ivory (blue-green) inlay and band (bottom).
Courtesy, American Craftsmen's Council, New York

BOWL. Robert G. Trout. Hand-carved, cocobolo wood.
Photo, Marshall LaCour

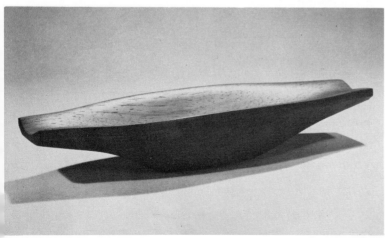

HANGING WEED POT. Robert G. Trout. Cocobolo wood.
Photo, Marshall LaCour

SHAVING MIRROR. Bernard Maas. Oiled walnut. The base was turned on a lathe; the upper portion was shaped with disk and drum sanders.
Photo, Lou Krone

WALNUT PIPE RACK; STONEWARE BOTTLE WITH ROSEWOOD
HANDLE. Bernard Maas.

Photo, Lou Krone

JEWELRY BOX. Robert G. Trout. Teak.
Photo, Marshall LaCour

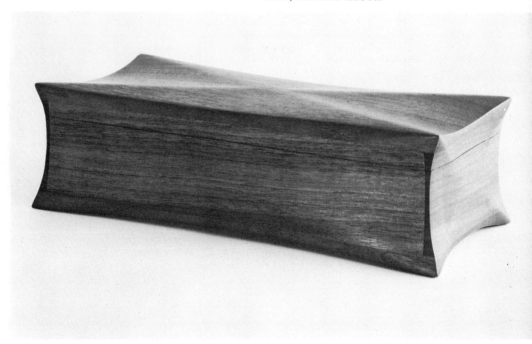

WEED POT. Robert G. Trout. Vermilion wood with cast sterling silver at top and bottom.
Photo, Marshall LaCour

COVERED CONTAINER. Robert G. Trout. Teak and silver.
Photo, Marshall LaCour

COVERED BOWL. Robert G. Trout. Turned teak with bonduc inlay.
Photo, Marshall LaCour

WINE RACK. Eben Warren Haskell. Walnut.

Courtesy, artist

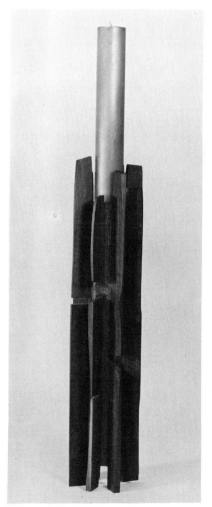

CHANDELIER. William A. Keyser, Jr. Walnut and aluminum. 36″ in diameter.

Courtesy, artist

CARVED WALNUT CANDLESTICK. William A. Keyser, Jr. 18″ high.

Courtesy, artist

Carved Bed and Chairs. J. B. Blunk. Redwood.

Bed: Collection, Mr. and Mrs. Gifford Phillips,
Santa Monica, California.
Photos: Courtesy, The Egg and The Eye
Gallery, Los Angeles

chapter 10

Furniture

With industrialization and mass production gripping the world, chairs, cabinets, tables, beds, and other useful objects are designed so they can be made economically by manufactured processes. Individualized, one-of-a-kind pieces of furniture are almost an anachronism.

Yet a few artists have persisted in creating custom pieces of furniture for an elite clientele. Some have eventually sold their designs to industry. But most often, mass-produced furniture designs emanate from the drawing boards of industrial designers who have been trained to create pieces that fit the concepts of mass production. So scarce are sculpture-trained furniture designers that those who have been successful have enjoyed publicity in arts, crafts, and interior-design publications, thus emphasizing the public's inability to draw a line between these disciplines.

Wharton Esherick of Paoli, Pennsylvania, originally a sculptor, has made a lifelong career of custom-built wood furniture. Whether Esherick creates an entire interior, a stairway, or a dictionary stand, it is conceived in sculptural terms. Esherick signs the original of each furniture piece, taking his cue from Chippen-dale, whose signed pieces are collector's items. Esherick emphasizes that the concept of completely handcrafted furniture is no longer valid. If power tools can do a job faster and better, by all means use them. The difference between a mass-produced piece and one made in the craftsman's workshop is that the latter supervises and also works on each piece individually.

A sculptor usually has very personal reasons for turning to furniture design. He may want something highly individual for his personal use. (That's how Esherick began. Though an artist, he made furniture that was admired and purchased by friends, until he became so busy he gave up sculpture and painting.) He may be commissioned to create furniture by an individual or as a compatible art form for an architectural plan. He may create furniture forms that purposely defy tradition. In our technocratic machine age with its smooth, shiny, sleek ideas of form, an artist may cultivate and emphasize the value of natural, untreated materials.

Industry is just beginning to recognize the wisdom of tapping talents of artists for new concepts in design. In Scandinavia, Paris, and in New York and Philadelphia in the United

177

States, shows of one-of-a-kind furnishings by artists have met tremendous enthusiasm. One Paris show was exhibited at several major art museums in America and Europe.

A specialty show at the Louvre in Paris issued invitations to artists and painters to submit furniture that could be used in an apartment or house and be produced at prices competitive with similar furnishings. Among the pieces submitted were a spiral-based chair, a table with a base of tortured metal, a wall cabinet with hidden drawers, and other pieces that were delightfully imaginative and different, yet practical.

At California's Pasadena Art Museum, a show was held with a jury to pass on both crafts and manufactured designs. Crafts were devoted to the conception and execution of a piece by one person; manufactured designs consisted of work that revealed community expression. However, the line separating the two categories was so thin that the museum curator felt manufactured designs were just as important as the so-called "diversions."

Qualifications for judging such a show may vary widely. The juror with an eye for crafts sees different values from those of the industrial designer, who may reject some ex-

pressions of craft because of impracticability or even a "corny" quality.

What of the need for comfort in furniture? This might be of utmost importance to some jurors, while others may select a chair because it happens to have a visually pleasing design and fit in with an overall architectural expression. Even though some traditional English- and French-designed furniture is uncomfortable, such pieces are still purchased because people like their appearance, and create an environment with them.

Inspiration for furniture designs often comes from the wood itself. Esherick says a wind-stripped tree, a certain grain, or the shape of a log may suggest a form. An Italian furniture designer points out: "A knot in a piece of wood can be the starting point for the design of a table or cupboard. An offcut found on a carpenter's bench can be combined with another to create a chair."

Current dictates that set a standard of dimensions by which everything from a bed to a bidet is cut perfectly, exactly, by machine, are a challenge to artistic ingenuity. The resources of the human mind, combined with inspiration and accidental happenings, are infinite and vital, and should be encouraged.

SIDEBOARD. Robert Charles Whitley. Hand-sculptured and carved walnut, top of catalpa wood. Interior is an antique glazed blue. Carved walnut lamp with a pine-ribbed, linen-paper-covered shade.

Courtesy, artist

The furniture maker uses sculptor's tools and techniques for many of his effects in wood. Here, Robert Charles Whitley uses a large push chisel. Worktable at back has wood lathe with various calipers, jigsaw, and machine-tool blades.

Courtesy, artist

Creating the panels for the walnut sideboard on page 178. The antique pull plane in the foreground is no longer available, but it is an indispensable tool for Whitley. Boards of rare wood used in cabinetmaking are at rear, including a large oak board with burl grain.

Courtesy, artist

DICTIONARY STAND. Robert Charles Whitley. Walnut, hand-sculpted and carved. Oil finished.

Courtesy, artist

DOUBLE MUSIC STAND. Sam Maloof.

Courtesy, The Egg and The Eye Gallery, Los Angeles

DICTIONARY STAND. Wharton Esherick. Uprights of cherry-wood; shelves of cottonwood.

Courtesy, artist

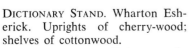

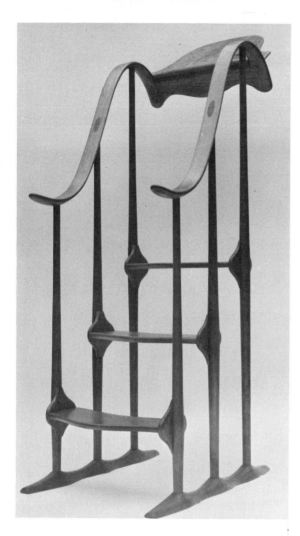

LIBRARY STEPS. Robert Charles Whitley. Wild cherry-wood.
Courtesy, artist

LIBRARY STEPS. Wharton Esherick.
Courtesy, artist

MUSIC STAND AND CHAIR. Wharton Esherick.
Courtesy, artist

SKYSCRAPER PEOPLE. Mike Nevelson. Painted wood. 71" high. 23 drawers in each. The human figure is adapted to furniture in an ingenious manner that combines sculpture and functionalism.

All photos: courtesy, artist

SEATED FIGURE. Mike Nevelson.
Pine and birch. 4' high.

LITTLE BOY WITH 5 DRAWERS.
Mike Nevelson.

PORTRAIT OF MR. AND MRS. COL-
LECTOR. Mike Nevelson. Pine. 6'
high.

THE AMERICAN HOUSE. Mike
Nevelson. Shingled storage cabinet.
6' high.

184

CHEST OF DRAWERS. William A. Keyser,
Jr. Teak. 40″ high, 15″ wide, 15″ deep.
Courtesy, American Craftsmen's Council,
New York

CHAIR AND CRADLE. Frank Rohloff. Chair,
of Japanese birch and cherry-wood, is a
modern interpretation of the early American ladder back. Observe the pegged construction in the cradle.

Courtesy, artist

HARPSICHORD. Robert Buecker and Ralph White. 1966. The artists, one a sculptor and one a painter, create one-of-a-kind harpsichords that critics consider an art form in furniture. They are based on the sixteenth-century Italian tradition of instrument design in many technical ways. The woods used for the body are maple and birch, with exotic woods for the keyboard; the ribs are basswood, whitewood, and pine.

Courtesy, Richard Feigen Gallery,
New York.
Photo, Scott Hyde

SNACK TABLE. William A. Keyser, Jr. Walnut plywood, molded. 18″ high.

Courtesy, artist

PIANO BENCH. Wendell Castle. Cherry-wood. Adjusts from 18″ to 24″ in height.

Courtesy, American Craftsmen's Council,
New York

FANTASY FURNITURE

Fantasy in furniture may be traced back to the ancient Egypt of five-thousand years ago. Man has always taken delight in fantasy, and even in ancient civilizations, furniture, or some of the fanciful decorations of it, acquired human and animal forms. There were angular sphinx, griffon, and chimera ornamentations that served as a change from classical designs.

The few artists who create fantasy furniture describe their work as a highly individual experience without regard to environment. They reject modern stylization and the industrial execution of furniture. Their results may be metaphoric, symbolic, or surrealistic, but all have a sculptural quality that is at times capricious, whimsical, or macabre. All pieces are functional as furniture.

Two Lovers. Thomas Simpson. 1966. Painted pine. A fantastic form with a fantastic clock that can't keep a straight face also has a music box.

Courtesy, artist

Neckrest. Sepik River Course, New Guinea. Wood, bamboo, shell, traces of polychrome. 16⅝" long. Fantasy forms are evident in the furniture of many primitive cultures.

Courtesy, Art Institute of Chicago

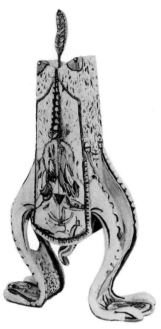

MAN BALANCING A FEATHER ON HIS NOSE. Thomas Simpson. 1967. Painted pine. This cabinet opens up to provide storage. The idea is from a nursery rhyme.
Courtesy, artist

CARVED CHAIRS. Pedro Friedeberg. 1967.
Courtesy, Ontario East Gallery, Chicago

CHAIR FOR SUITE. Kate Millett. 1965. 2¾' high.

TABLE SETTING FOR THE SUITE. Kate Millett. 1965.
Courtesy, artist

HOLY, HOLY, HOLY, THE WHOLE EARTH IS FULL OF HIS GLORY. Milton Horn. Ark reredos in the University Hospital, All Faiths Chapel, West Virginia University, Morgantown. Carved directly in limbawood. 11′ high overall. Fabric ark cover woven to simulate wood grain.

Architects, C. E. Silling and Associates.
Photo, Estelle Horn

chapter 11

Wood, the Artist, and the Architect

The use of wood in architecture for function and decoration is universal and ancient. While the purposes have not changed, the ways in which wood has been utilized in contemporary architecture have. Imaginative church design is probably most responsible for these changes in the past few decades. The ingenuity and innovations and the use of natural materials fostered by the Bauhaus and adapted by such architectural giants as Frank Lloyd Wright, Le Corbusier, and others have also been responsible.

However, the relationship between architect and artist-craftsman during the twentieth century has been at best an uneasy one. Except in the case of religious architecture, sculpture and painting play a secondary and even negligible role in contemporary architectural expression. In the few buildings where the work of the sculptor or muralist is seen, the artist has too often been called in after the structure has been completed, and his work was added as an afterthought. The result was often weak and ineffectual.

Among younger architects, a more sophisticated attitude toward a collaboration with the artist, from drawing board to completion, is slowly emerging. The artist, once resentful of his work being considered only a decorative addition, finds that a more realistic view now exists concerning collaboration with an architect. His work can be both expressive and decorative when placed in a setting about which he feels a strong conviction. When both the architect's and the artist's aims are fundamentally the same, both stand to profit from mutual understanding and respect.

A contemporary theory is that architecture that provides shelter and three-dimensional space in which man lives, works, and worships should also be concerned with his values. Sculpture, mosaics, murals, and other fine art forms can enable man to relate to his architecture through scale, color, and symbols. The ideal, then, is to provide comprehensive total expression of man's values through the coalition of art and architecture.

The practical problems, however, become more fundamental: Where does the architect find an artist-craftsman who has a knowledge of the builder's problems and who won't insist that art form is more important than structural form? Where can the architect see work of various artists and find one with a personality whose objectives will be compatible with his aims? And will the client accept the artist's work and costs?

Successful alliances between architect and artist are becoming evident in new buildings, which proves that practical questions are not insoluble. Research may be required; and the artist must let architects know he is available and what his talents are. In the end, the architectural structure is furnished with objects that meet the architect's esthetic demands; the artist, consequently, is displaying his work; and the client has a unique building enhanced with individually created objects that often have prestige value and bring him publicity.

THE SCARLET LETTER AND THE RAVEN. Stanley Kaplan. Mural for a high school library combines the characters of a classic novel and a poem.

Courtesy, artist

FOOTBALL MURAL. Stanley Kaplan. Carved in Philippine mahogany planks glued together. 42″ × 120″. Polychromed with oil stains and gold leaf (Mike Manuche's Restaurant, New York).

Courtesy, artist

Stanley Kaplan's mural creations have their beginning when 1″ pieces of Philippine mahogany boards are edge-glued and clamped together. Kaplan says, "Wood is an extremely flexible medium for artistic expression and, in its plank form, the sculptural and painting possibilities are challenging for inventive spatial creations."

Kaplan outlines the design on the glued raw-wood planks with tempera colors. Then he chisels away the bas-relief or background areas. He applies stains to highlight the carvings, seals the wood, and then proceeds to paint. The finished mural is a wedding of painting and wood carving. There is a play between areas that are high and low, flat and smooth, light and dark, stained and colored.

MOSES AND BEZALEL. Milton
Horn. Appalachian oak. 7' high.
Carefully selected planks are laminated. The direct carving is based
on the symbolism of the Halakah
and the Haggada. Holy Ark doors
in the B'nai Israel Temple, Charles-
ton, West Virginia.

Photo, Estelle Horn

Milton Horn, an internationally known
Chicago sculptor, has worked with architects in
many types of buildings. He points out some of
the problems involved in an architectural al-
liance that the artist is expected to solve.

Primarily, he cautions, no two jobs present the same set of situations. Each must be
studied, evaluated, and the individual solutions discovered. Though the problems in one
project may never appear in another, yet you
learn from each one.

Scale must be developed. From how far away will the piece have to be seen and from what angles? Perspective can be very complex. For example, in a commission for a two-story wall in a bank, the head of a figure, if seen from an even plane, is not in proportion to the body. Yet, seen from below, looking up, the enlarged head actually appears to be the proper size for the body. As a work of art, the piece must have a form and expressiveness . . . even a mythical quality. It must speak with the people, not to them or at them.

If the piece must function, as in a church, how it will be used and by whom must be taken into consideration. In developing an Ark for a temple, Mr. Horn had to be sure the rabbi could reach the opening to remove and place the scrolls conveniently.

With wood, factors of humidity and temperature must be studied. In mounting a mural or placing an altarpiece, room must be allowed for the wood to expand, for air to circulate, and other technical aspects. In essence, the artist must be like the myriad-minded man of the Renaissance, and know much more than his art form: he must also understand the problems of the architect, the engineer, the botanist, and be able to cope with any other discipline that presents itself for the successful completion of the project.

Detail from MOSES AND BEZALEL (at left), by Milton Horn, shows how the planks are glued so the lines of lamination barely show. The intricate carving changes direction with the grain of each 2″ laminated board, and is expertly done. Horn uses only the chisel and gouge; he does no sandpapering or rasping.

Photo, Estelle Horn

THE ANGEL OF FIRE (detail). Milton Horn. From the HOLY, HOLY, HOLY carving, page 188. Angel at upper left.

Photo, Estelle Horn

INDIAN DOOR: TREE OF LIFE (half only).

CHINESE DOOR (half only).

EGYPTIAN DOOR (half only).

ASSYRIAN DOOR (half only).

FRENCH DOOR. All carvings of World Doors are by Chinese artist-craftsmen and are installed in the General Time Corporation building, Stamford, Connecticut. There are 19 such doors set into archways. They are made of teak, and represent the various countries of the world.

Photos, Robert Wendlinger

MEMORIAL WALL. Sam Russo. Wood, gessoed and painted with gold leaf and other colors. Dedicated to the memory of the Jews who perished under the Nazis. In the Temple Anshe Hesed, Erie, Pennsylvania.

Courtesy, artist

FIREPLACE PANEL. Mignonne Keller.
Carved limbawood. 8 separate pieces
mounted. 8′ high, 11″ wide. Dr. R.
B. Pelzel residence, Mercer Island,
Washington.

Paul Kirk, architect.
Photo, Elizabeth Green

PAIR OF DOOR PUSHES. Mignonne
Keller. Carved teak. 6″ × 22″ each.
Photo, William Eng

Preparing the wood and carving the panels for the fireplace
mounting. Because of the long narrow shape, the artist tried to
avoid a totem-like effect. She developed her design as she worked
the eight separate pieces of wood.

Courtesy, artist.
Photos, Elizabeth Green

ELEVATOR PANELS. Mignonne Keller. Carved walnut. Building at 1411 4th Avenue, Seattle, Washington.

Architects, Bassetti and Morse, AIA.

Photo, Elizabeth Green

PAIR OF CARVED DOOR HANDLES. Mignonne Keller. Sakar. Home of Dr. and Mrs. Charles Fine, Bellevue, Washington.

Courtesy, artist

DOOR. Kathy Haun. Solid mahogany, carved.

Courtesy, artist

DOOR IN DEPTH. Rudy Seno. Constructed from plywood and ready-made moldings and turnings. The two center doors within the door may be opened. May be used as a door or piece of decorative furnishing.

DOOR AND STAIRCASE. Carved interior door panels offset the stark simplicity of the doors and wooden banister.

Architect, William Koster, Cleveland, Ohio

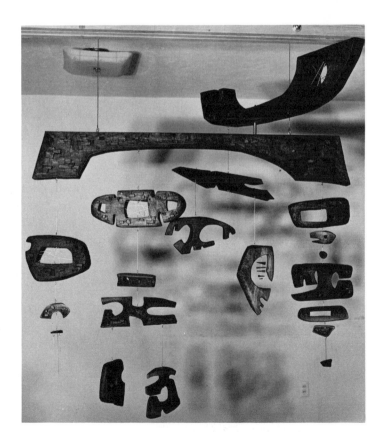

SUSPENDED SCULPTURE. Kathy Haun. Walnut with brass and wire, developed as a hanging room divider.

Courtesy, artist

Our Lady of Mount Carmel Church, Asti, California.

Albert R. Hunter, Jr., AIA.
Courtesy, California Redwood Association, San Francisco

Concordia Lutheran Church, Kingsport, Tennessee.
Architect, Frank J. Martin and Associates.
Courtesy, California Redwood Association, San Francisco

St. Augustine's Episcopal Church, Gary, Indiana.
Architect, Edward D. Dart, AIA.
Courtesy, California Redwood Association, San Francisco.
Photo, Hedrich-Blessing

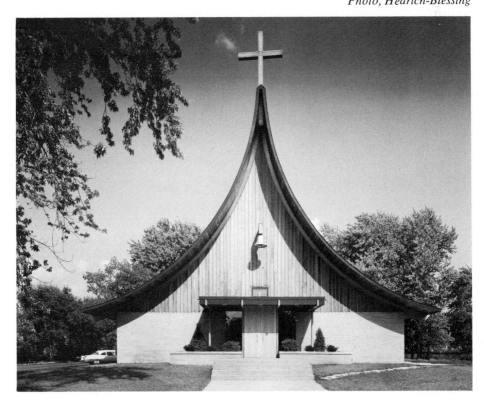

Furniture showroom, Sarasota, Florida. Glue-laminated redwood bents gracefully support circular areas of glass.

Courtesy, California Redwood Association, San Francisco.
Photo, Alexandre Georges

Redwood staircases for an interior and exterior.
Courtesy, California Redwood Association, San Francisco.
Photos, Dennis Galloway and Pete Kinch

Glossary

ANTICRAFTSMANSHIP

The philosophy and practice that rough, un-finished surfaces and haphazard joining methods are as valid as sleek finished surfaces and carefully carpentered joints.

ASSEMBLAGE

The technique of combining related or unrelated objects or scraps into an artistic arrangement.

BLEACHING

The process of removing natural or applied color from wood with a prepared acid solution.

BURL

Domelike outgrowth from a tree trunk caused by a broken or cut branch.

CAMBIUM

Layer of living cells of the inner surface of the bark that carries food from the leaves to all parts of the tree.

CARVING

The process of subtracting or taking away parts of the wood or other material and leaving a shape or design.

CHECK

The cracks that occur in a log radially from the center to the bark as the result of drying.

CHISEL

A metal tool with a straight cutting edge at the end of the blade.

CLAMP

A metal or wood device used to hold wood to a workbench or other surface while carving.

COMMON WOOD

Classification of lumber indicating less select quality of wood containing slight or great defects depending upon the grade.

CONSTRUCTIVISM

An artistic expression that arose after World War I, when materials were constructed as in architecture, and new ideas about volume and space emerged. Constructivism used concave and transparent forms. Later it became known as "Constructionism."

CROSSCUT

Cutting a board or log across the grain or in opposition to its fibrous structure.

CROTCH

V-like area of tree where branch and trunk separate; it possesses unusual grain patterns.

CUBISM

An art form that investigated esthetic elements by first fragmenting, and then reconstructing, objects and images in new visual forms.

CURE

To dry and preserve a log for future use.

DECORATIVE

An art form meant to be ornamental.

DIRECT CARVING

Creating sculpture by chiseling, gouging, or sawing a log or board: as opposed to constructing to create shape and volume.

DOWEL

A cylindrical wood rod used as a pin to join two pieces of wood together.

DRESSED BOARD

A length of wood that has been dried and planed on all sides.

END GRAIN ON A BOARD

The end pattern that is the result of a horizontal cut across a log, showing portions of the ring, pith, heartwood, and sapwood.

FACE GRAIN

The pattern of grain evident on the face, or length, of a dressed board.

FANTASY FURNITURE

A style of furniture design based on metaphor, symbolism, or decorative whimsy.

FIGURE

An unusual pattern in grain caused by unusual growth spurts in a tree.

FILE

A cutting tool with ridges used for smoothing wood.

FORM

In sculpture, the result of uniting many diverse elements, such as shape, line, texture, subject, mass, color, and so on, until clear relationships exist and each element functions as a consistent whole.

FRAGMENTATION

Cutting objects and reassembling the parts into a new relationship.

GLOSS

A shiny surface finish.

GOUGES

Metal tools with sharp blade edges in a variety of shapes from shallow *U*'s to deep *V*'s.

GRAIN

Actual fibrous structure of wood. The pattern of the grain is affected by the seasonal growth of the tree.

HARDWOOD

Classification of wood from trees with broad leaves. The grain is usually close.

HEARTWOOD

The tree growth surrounding the pith that once was sapwood; the heartwood gives the tree strength.

JOINTS

Places where wood of two or more pieces are put together by gluing, doweling, or use of other carpentering techniques such as dovetailing, tongue and groove, and so on.

KILN-DRYING

The proces of rapid-drying lumber by heat as opposed to air-drying over a long period of time.

KINETIC SCULPTURES

Those having one or more parts that move by use of motors or other mechanical devices.

KNOTS

Dark defects in wood caused by branches breaking off as the tree grew.

LAMINATING

Combining layers of wood by gluing.

LINEAR

Term used to describe elements of a sculpture that resemble the lines used in drawing techniques.

LUMBER

Wood that has been cut, dried, and dressed.

MALLET

A hardwood (usually lignum vitae) hammer-like tool used to drive the chisel or gouge into the wood.

MATTE

A dull surface finish.

NEGATIVE SPACE

Term used in sculpture to define the open spaces that allow "air" to penetrate the sculpture.

NONPURIST

One who rejects or adds to traditional methods and materials to achieve a desired result.

OILSTONE

A stone used with oil for sharpening tools.

ORGANIC FORMS

Those inspired by shapes of natural organic objects such as stones, algae, flower growth, root formations, and so on.

PITH

The dark center portion of the tree from which growth began.

PLUGGING

The technique of placing a wooden peg over a screw used to join woods.

PLYWOOD

Laminated sheets of wood consisting of three or more layers.

POLYCHROMED

Painted many colors.

POROUS WOODS

Another name for hardwoods, which frequently have vessels or pores large enough to be seen without magnification.

PRIMITIVE SCULPTURE

Carvings made by people of primitive cultures such as those in Africa, Samoa, New Guinea, and so on. The planes are usually simplified and stylized.

PURIST

One who adheres to traditional methods and materials.

RASP

A type of file with raised points that form the cutting surface, whereas a true file uses cutting ridges.

RELIEF

A carved or constructed design attached to a backing.

RIFFLERS

Small files and rasps shaped at each end.

RIPPING

Cutting a board or log with the grain and in the same direction as the fibrous structure.

ROUGH-SAWN WOOD

Boards cut from a log before planing and dressing.

SAPWOOD

The growth layers that carry sap from the roots to the leaves.

SEALING

The process of covering the pores of a log to prevent too rapid drying. Also, the process of closing the pores with varnish, shellac, or other paint sealer to prevent painted color from entering the wood.

SELECT WOOD

A classification of lumber that indicates high-quality, blemish-free grades.

SOFTWOOD

A classification of wood from trees that have needlelike leaves. Softwoods usually have large and open grains.

STAINING

The process of changing the natural color of a wood by adding color pigment to the pores of the wood (as opposed to painting, where the color pigment lies on top of wood that has been sealed).

TEXTURE

The surface quality of a material that one can feel or see.

TRUTH TO MATERIALS

The idea that inherent qualities of a material should either be used or ignored, and not camouflaged or made to look like another material.

WARPAGE

Tendency of wood to curve or twist out of shape as the result of uneven drying or exposure to moisture.

WEATHERED WOOD

Scrap pieces from trees or used lumber that have been exposed to natural elements of air, sun, moisture, and so on.

Index

A

Accessories, 162–175
Accorsi, William, 163
Acetylene torch, 3
American carvings, 3, 4
Anderson, Jeremy, 151
Anderson, John, 84, 85
Animal form, 108–113
Annual rings, 36
Anticraftsmanship, 69, 88
Archipenko, Alexander, 57
Architecture, 188–203
Arman, 135
Arnold, Anne, 21, 58, 64, 79, 107, 110, 112
Arp, Jean, 15, 18, 29
Assemblage, 11, 30, 120–135

B

Band saw, 6, 50, 51, 74, 128, 138
Barlach, Ernest, 14, 18
Barnes, Roger, 148
Barr, 36, 41
Baskin, Leonard, 22, 101, 103, 108
Baum, Don, 27
Beal, Sondra, 29, 60, 86
Bladen, Ronald, 153
Bleaching wood, 59, 60, 61
Blunk, J. B., 176
Borcherdt, Fred, 7, 40, 68, 90, 96, 114, 165
Bourgeois, Louise, 134
Bowl, turning, 168, 169
Bowls, demonstrations of, 166–169
Brancusi, Constantin, 13, 14, 29
Buecker, Robert, 185
Burck, Jacob, 134
Burl, 36, 179
Burning wood, 128, 138, 140, 141, 166

C

Calder, Alexander, 15, 57, 163
Camargo, Sergio, 142

CAMBIUM, 36
CARDENAS, AUGUSTIN, 24
CARPENTER, STANLEY L., 120
CARVING, 90–119
CARVING TOOLS, 92, 93, 94
CASTLE, WENDELL, 185
CATLETT, ELIZABETH, 102
CHAIN SAW, 4, 40, 44, 45
CHASE, DORIS, 33, 87
CHECK, 3, 4, 39, 41
CHERULLO, ARNOLD, 10, 152, 155
CHISELS, gouges, 45, 71, 92, 93, 94
CLAMPS, 93, 94
COLE, NATALIE, 65
COLOR, natural wood, 38
COLORING WOOD, 58
CONSTRUCTIONS
    relief, 136–145
    three-dimensional, 146–159
CONSTRUCTIVISM, 14, 29
COUNTERSINKING, 76, 77
CRAFTSMANSHIP, 69
CROSSCUTTING, 43
CROTCH, 36
CUBISM, 14, 18, 29

D

DADAISTS, 18
DAGG, RALPH NOEL, facing 151
D'HAESE, ROEL, 23˙
DIRUBE, ROLAND LÓPEZ, 148, 154
DOWELS, 6, 9, 46, 77, 79, 120, 167
DRAW KNIFE, 43
DRESSED LUMBER, 38, 39
DRILL PRESS, 52, 53
DRILLS, portable, 55
DRUCKS, MICHAEL, 133
DRYING AND SEALING, 41
DUBIN, WILLIAM, 88

E

EDGE AND END GLUING, 74, 75
EMOTIONS, 3, 22, 26, 121
END GRAIN, 36, 37
EPOXY RESIN, 68, 69

ESHERICK, WHARTON, 177, 178, 180, 181
ESHOO, ROBERT, 143

F

FANTASY FURNITURE, 186, 187
FARALLA, JAMES, 25
FEDEROFF, GEORGE, 171
FIGURE, 36–39
   animal, 108–113
   human, 100–107
FOGEL, JACQUELINE, 41, 56, 132, facing 150
FOREST PRODUCTS LABORATORY, 57
FORM, animal, 108–113
FOUR, VICTOR, 60
FRAGMENTATION, 6
FRAZIER, CHARLES, 156
FRIDEBERG, PEDRO, 162, 187
FULFORD, PATRICIA, 149
FURNITURE, 176–187
   fantasy, 186, 187
FUTURISTS, 14

G

GAUGIN, EMILE, 104
GLASER, JERRY, 171
GLUE GUN, electric, 69
GLUING, 66–75
GOODYEAR, JOHN, 156
GOUGES, chisels, 45, 71, 92–94
GRAIN, 36–39
GREEN, ALAN, 143
GROSS, CHAIM, 16, 18, 19, 21, 63, 91
GWYTHER, IRWIN, 144

H

HARDWOOD, 35, 42
HASKELL, EBEN WARREN, 171, 175
HAUN, KATHY, 198, 199
HEARTWOOD, 36, 37, 41, 75
HEPWORTH, BARBARA, 19, 20, 27
HOKANSON, HANS, 26, 155
HOLLOWING, 41
HORN, MILTON, 95, 188, 192, 193

HOSTETLER, DAVID, frontispiece, 37, 41, 45, 58, 93, 105
HUMAN FIGURE, 100–107

I

INDIANA, ROBERT, 127
INLAY, 164, 167
INSTITUTE OF DESIGN, 5, 6, 46, 47, 49–53

J

JENSON, LEO, 61
JIG SAW, 8, 50, 51, 74
JOHNSON, MELVIN, 158
JOHNSTON, YNEZ, 88
JOINING WOOD, 66–89

K

KABOT, JOHN RANDALL, 10
KAPLAN, STANLEY, facing 118, 190, 191
KEARNEY, JOHN W., 64
KELLER, MIGNONNE, 197, 198
KEYSER, WILLIAM A., 175, 184, 185
KINETIC, 29, 84–86
KNOTS, 36, 37
KOESTER, RALPH, 144
KOHN, GABRIEL, 28, 66
KOWAL, DENNIS, 117
KOWAL, RICHARD, facing 151

L

LAKAKIS, MICHAEL, 156
LAMINATING, 23, 28–30, 33, 37, 66–75, 163
    demonstration, 69–71
LANGLAIS, BERNARD, 11, 30, facing 119, 124, 125, 131
LARSON, EDWARD S., 102
LATHE, 48, 49, 166, 168, 169
LAURENS, HENRI, 14, 18, 57
LINE, 137
LITTLE, JOHN, facing 118
LOCKHART, ROBERT, 109, 111, 112
LOGS
    carving, 40, 41, 91
    finding, 40
    sealing and drying, 41
LÓPEZ-GARCÍA, ANTONIO, 63

M

MAAS, BERNARD, 172, 173
MAJOROWICZ, ROGER, 107
MALOOF, SAM, 180
MARISOL, 58, 157
MEILACH, DONA, 127, 133
MILLETT, KATE, 187
MOORE, HENRY, 17–20
MUÑOZ, LUCIO, 31
MURALS, 190, 191

N

NADELMAN, ELIE, 57, 101
NEVELSON, LOUISE, 21, 31, 58, 126
NEVELSON, MIKE, 83, 87, 150, 182, 183
NICHOLSON, BEN, 20, 142
NON-REPRESENTATIONAL STATEMENTS, 114–119

O

ONDERDONK, FORMAN, 28, 61, 78, facing 118, 146
ORIENTAL SCULPTURE, 4
OXYACETYLENE TORCH, 138, 141

P

PACKARD, DAVID, 155
PAINT, types of, 58
PAINTING AND FINISHING WOOD, 57–61
PEARSON, RAY, 5, 6, 46–53
PEGGING, 66–89, 167
PICASSO, PABLO, 13, 14, 57, 163
PIERRON, ROBERT, facing 119, 123, 128–130, 138–142
PITH, 36
PLAIN SAWED, 39
PLUGGING, 76, 77
PORTABLE POWER TOOLS, 54
POWELL, FRED, 115
POWER TOOLS, 43–55, 166–169
PRESTINI, JAMES, 8, 9, 24
PRIMEAU, CLAUDE, 2, 106, 119
PRIMITIVE SCULPTURE, 12, 13, 16, 59, 91, 100, 108–110, 164, 165, 186
PURISM, 57, 122

Q

Quartered sawed, 39

R

Ramírez, Eduardo, 62, 151
Relief constructions, 136–145
Rift sawed, 39
Rohloff, Frank, 184
Rothenstein, Michael, 131
Russell, James, 65, 145
Russo, Sam, 196

S

Safety rules
    carving, 96
    portable tools, 55
    power tools, 43, 44
Sanders, 55
Sandmann, Herbert, 62
Sapwood, 4, 36, 37, 41, 75
Saw
    band, 6, 50, 51, 74, 128, 138
    chain, 4, 40, 44, 45
    jig, 8, 50, 51, 74
    table, 5, 46, 47
Scrap wood, 11, 25, 30, 40, 41, 120–135
Sculptural constructions, 146–159
Sealing and drying, 41
Selecting and buying wood, 38–40
Seno, Rudy, 198
Shanker, L., 149
Sharpening tools, 94–95
Shredding wood, 128, 130
Sildar, William P., 30–83, 85
Simon, Sidney, 23, 61, 82, 95, 102, 106, 118, 134
Simpson, Thomas, 186, 187
Skaling, Audrey, 86, 143
Smith, David, 147
Smoothing, 61
Softwood, 35, 42
Solomon, Masha, 118
Sovetski, Bunni, 22, 103, 104
Stahly, François, 34

STAINING, 58
STOCKSDALE, ROBERT, 168–170
STRETCHING WOOD, 8, 9
SUGARMAN, GEORGE, 89, 159
SURFACE FINISHING, 58–61
SUVERO, MARK DI, 150

T

TABLE SAW, 46, 47
TABLE SAW SCULPTURE, 5
TAKAHASHI, KIYOSHI, 106
THREE-DIMENSIONAL CONSTRUCTIONS, 146–159
TOMANY, GERALD J., frontispiece, 68, 70, 72, 73
TOOLS
    hand and power, 43
    hand carving, 92, 93, 94
    sharpening, 94, 95
TOWNLEY, HUGH, 84
TOWNSEND, JOHN, 136
TRACHSLER, DON, facing 150, 153
TRANSPARENT FINISHES, 58
TREE GROWTH, 35–37
TROLLER, FRED, 152
TROUT, ROBERT G., facing 151, 164, 167, 171–174
TRUTH OF MATERIALS, 41, 57
TURNING, bowl, 168, 169

U

ULRICH, MARK, 113
URBAN, MYCHAJLO R., 114, 116, 119, facing 150
U.S. DEPARTMENT OF AGRICULTURE
    Forest Products Laboratory, 57

V

VRANA, ALBERT, 98, 99

W

WAGEMAKER, JAAP, 123
WAXING AND OILING, 60
WEATHERED WOOD, 11, 25, 30, 40, 41, 120–135
WEINBERG, ELBERT, 102, 107
WEINER, EGON, 97
WESTERMANN, H. C., 32, 152, 154

WHITE, RALPH, 64, 185
WHITLEY, ROBERT C., facing 118, 178–181
WILLENBECHER, JOHN, 144
WISEMAN, ANNE, 133
WOJCIK, GARY, 116
WOOD, GRADES, 38, 39
WOOD SELECTION CHART, 42